HISTORY AND PHILOSOPHY
OF
CAODAISM

Gabriel GOBRON

HISTORY AND PHILOSOPHY

OF

CAODAISM

Reformed Buddhism, Vietnamese Spiritism,
New Religion in Eurasia

Translated from the original French by Phạm-xuân-Thái

Published under the auspices of His Excellency Trần-quang-Vinh, Major-General, Commander-in-Chief of the Caodaist Troops, Minister of the Armed Forces of the Government of Vietnam

INTRODUCTION

Gabriel Gobron, author of the present work on Caodaism, was an ardent and courageous writer, journalist and lecturer. Born at Bayonville (Meurthe-et-Moselle), July 5, 1895, he quit the world and its sufferings at Rethel, July 8, 1941. With the present work and undoubtedly with others that shall follow, Gabriel Gobron continues his literary works in the Beyond. This time, the work far surpasses literature.

We can speak of the « Message » and with a capital letter.

Being an eminent polyglot, an indefatigable inquirer in the world of the Spirit and spirits, novelist, historian, journalist and teacher, Gabriel was a curious man and himself a curiosity. A Great soul, by his overflowing intellectual generosity, he was an ardent polemicist.

He was curious indeed, but without dilettantism: when he thought to have discovered a spiritual beauty, a philosophical or religious truth, he liked to make it known and shared by others at once. He would not hesitate to fight, always with passion, against those, who, in his eyes, wanted to put the light under a bushel. It is in this way that he discovered Caodaism, and also in this way that he fought to his last breath, praying for his illumination. Gabriel Gobron, a great intellect, was above all a great heart.

After a period of research, study and discovery beginning in 1930, Gabriel Gobron became a convinced propagator, a well-informed, and before long officially accredited initiator of Caosdaism in the West and more particularly in France.

Lectures, articles and observations succeeded one another, and with the remaining unpublished texts, they form a copious collection of which the present posthumous book is one of the main parts.

Thus the present work constitutes an authentic message from the Beyond. It was a consoling task to us to work out this text.

« A Message from Heaven » this posthumous work, we are sure, will be particularly honored by the numerous spiritist friends of the author who has done so much, by his pen, speech and experimentation, for spiritism.

His printed works number ten volumes and hundred articles or published essays everywhere, in the world, in the languages which he spoke and wrote besides French : English, German, Italian, Spanish and Portuguese.

Gabriel Gobron, being the author of several novels, had written a great many rustic pages about the life of the workers in country and city.

Truly, Gabriel Gobron was a delicate, sensitive, even tender soul, who very often hid himself voluntarily behind this rude aspect in the manner of Léon Bloy.

This secret sensibility of the heart and the soul had more than once inspired pages of remarkable delicacy and finesse.

Delicate and modest tenderness, reaction of the romantic poet who would not deny the little blue flower of popular romance or the archaic complaints of a folklore which he loved.

Having exhausted himself writing big books inspired by the petty miseries of daily bourgeois life, like Henri Heine, he could write little songs from a wealth of painful experience.

It is certain that Gabriel Gobron, throughout his lifetime, was a rebel, a non-conformist, an « outsider », like Théo Varlet and Macolm Mac-Laren, the poets whom he liked and had made acquaintance with at the Mercure Universel. Along with and in his scholastic, historic and journalistic works, we find irritated, nervous and bitter pages to the point of crying out and invective. They have been called « quibbling and rancor », but the truth is that : all Gabriel Gobron's works imbued with truth and suffering life, belong to the literary class which is so rightly named Dolorism of which Julien Teppe is the founder.

The style and the rhythm of the sentences of the writer, Gabriel Gobron, adapt themselves spontaneously to the subject treated.

The style and the form adapt themselves to the sentiments to such a point as to appear unequal and different, and the general impression given is that no professional machinery has presided over the composition of this work, which grew up freely and courageously, like nature in its liberty, with thick copses and fine glades.

Gabriel Gobron seems to be aided in the completion of his work by one of those sorceresses painted by Brenghel-le-Jeune, who mix and blend the best with the worst, the most diverse and repulsive ingredients. The pot boils, the lid is lifted, and Gabriel Gobron, the writer, is not satisfied with the veracity of the facts simply recounted : he must pose in the most direct terms, he delights in the densest materials as much by the style adopted as by the vocabulary employed.

I considered « Notre Dame des Neiges » (1) to be a great philosophical document in which a man expresses himself without constraint, even esthetically, and without any trace of social hypocrisy. Whether it pleases or not, the fact is : the man frees himself by writing, and the present case, it not only concerns an individual deliberation, but numerous heredities which, tired of being repelled or sublimated, express themselves.

Thus, the « beings » which exist in man, free themselves from constraints, injustices imposed by life : social, individual, collective, economic injustices, etc... And at bottom, in the very depths, but real, animated, tenacious and captivating, the mystic torture of the soul which needs God and justice, cries out : « Blessed are they which do hunger and thirst after righteousness, for they shall be filled » (2).

The « Messages » received by certain attentive and receptive mediums, prove that Gabriel Gobron is now among those who are satisfied.

The social and economic injustices, the oppressions of the rich against the poor, and the wrongs of one and the other, are rudely handled in the various works of Gabriel Gobron among others, in « Les Couarrails de Pont-à-Mousson » published by Berger-Levrault and in « Barbandouille » Mercure Universel and in « Tournemol », a novel about a bad professor.

In these works, Gabriel Gobron does not proceed by allusion ; his style is direct, loaded with invective. He insists rigorously on the facts that he has exposed, but he also speaks frankly about the reforms and transformations of present society, of which he anticipates the corruption and degeneration to mediocrity.

Let me cite anew the preface of the study of 1938, which exposes the « case » of Gabriel Gobron.

---

(1) Some Copies of this fine book are still to be found at : Mme Vve G. Gobron, 9, rue de Serre, à Nancy (Meurthe-et-Moselle).
(2) Extract from the preface by Valentin Bresle, founder and director of the Mercure Universel, 12, rue Fromentin, Paris (9e).

It is the « case », because Gabriel Gobron is a gentle lamb, who endeavours in vain to become enraged, whence the attitude of vituperation, which makes us think of (as I have mentioned above) Léon Bloy and of the Old Testament prophets.

Gabriel Gobron is a mild man and his dreams are magnificent :

« And we were dreaming, since our primary school days, to learn how to teach the little people of the world, to create a « Cosmis Home » by the side of the « House of God » ! Do not make teaching an immediate, utilitarian business and materialistic matter, but make education bio-cosmic to show the students that we are as much the glorious sons of the Universe as the obscure children of the hamlets ! Reveal the divine that slumber in us, the subconscious by which we are in relation with the most improbable and mysterious entities and occult faculties, and which assures the triumph of the Spirit over animality, over the brute that growls within us !

Reveal the divine that slumbers within us, and seek again for God as much as God seeks us, Then it will be possible to envisage the fusion of the « House of God » and the « Cosmic Home » into an immense Fraternal Temple, the synthesis of both.

We are still far from this harmony of the mystic ; we are still far from it as much through the fault and incomprehension of some, the dogmatics, as of others, the rationalists. The « House of God » and the « Cosmic Home » will still be opposed to each other for a long time to come. They are, however, the fraternal and permanent expression of the « ad Deum » which is in the heart of all human beings, living tabernacles of the divine.

The book of Gabriel Gobron is crammed with just, interesting, and elevated ideas on education to be given, on liberty to be respected, and on spirituality, etc... His literary form is then more serene, sober and harmonious ; it is an immense sheet of water, limpid and fresh before the dam and torrential rapids and the overflowing of the crude polemic style.

We must defend « Jean Peuple », we must protect the exploited from exploitation, but we must not let « Jean Peuple » think that he is a little saint, for as soon as a « Jean Peuple » happens to be on the other side... we quickly find that power corrupts.

Therefore, while he defends him, at the same time Gabriel Gobron exposes the manias, vices and misunderstandings of this good « Jean Peuple ».

And it's too bad for the too fond ears, for which the « ostendite testes » of Saint Bernard must be translated into « Be Men » for fear of a literal translation.

Gabriel Gobron writes, « Vanquish animality, conquer the brute that growls in us », and by his style, he, the new Doctor Jekyll, lets Mr. Hyde whom all of us bear in us, speak freely. But as in Stevenson novel, it happens that Mr. Hyde disengages himself from the wise Doctor Jekyll, we may then ask ourselves whether Gabriel Gobron would not have too fixed a tendency to separate forceably matter from spirit. The Brute is what it is, useful and capable of perfection destined to transmute itself, to evolve and elevate itself from heavy planes to the ethereal, It is thus for example, that he speaks rudely of sexuality and even of sensuality, initiated in the secrets of Stanislas of Guaita. Gabriel Gobron knows well that the human center of « G » of the sacred Pentagram bears precisely on him, all the possibilities of evolution, and of transformation on all planes : cosmic, carnal, mystic and divine. By the letter « G », matter exalts and purifies itself toward the spirit, the spirit incarnated in matter. The whole forms one (1).

Beside their literary and philosophical merits, the works of Gabriel Gobron constitute and contain some psychological documents. They have been the expression of social retrogressions of several generations. This was true of some books of our author.

Injustices borne, sincere and pure dreams unrealized, atavistic restraints, all the accumulated hereditary traits, these are what the author relates to us, for the author is urged by a thousand demon-inspirers, who blow us the best and the worst in the long genealogy, which Gabriel Gobron gives us.

He sometimes touches grandeur while his simplicity shows what it is and what he is. But soon Mr. Hyde returns and here is our author, lost in massive details, which, however, may have their own significance and reasons for existence.

The reader, tasting the paragraphs of a very good observation (where harmonized sensibility dominates the style and simplifies it), tells to himself that the dispersion, the loss of self-control, the ebullience of the atavistic rancors really constitute, with « the pride of being what he is », the psychological document, about which I have spoken ; and the author is the actor at the same time, though without acting or posing in the « Human Comedy ».

---

(1) *Valentin Bresle has since greatly developed these esderic theories in* Thesaurus magiæ *and in* Thesaurus Sapentiæ.

This must be said because in the present posthumous work, the « History and Philosophy of Caodaism », the psychological case is surpassed : the present work is a metapsychic testimony.

These are no more the deceased ancestors of Gabriel Gobron expressing themselves through him as a literary medium, but rather Grabriel Gobron himself, the Brother Gago from the Eternal Orient, who gives us his message. The present book is a precious testimony and, may we venture to say, a fundamental book, the spiritual repercussions of which will be considerable.

The word Caodaism derives from Cao-Dai, the literal translation of which corresponds to : Supreme Palace. This double term is found in the most ancient buddhist prayers. It establishes the principal origin of this religion, which is first of all, as we shall see, a kind of reformed Buddhism.

The new religion (its essential message dates from 1926) is rooted in the most tried tradition of Buddhism, and its purest revelations.

Caodaism, is, up to a certain point, comparable to what Protestantism had been in its origin, compared to Catholicism. For the rest, even this possibility of comparison is already outweighed in the beneficent sense, that is to say, in the sense of good understanding. Permitting the vision in a more or less remote future, the union of the christian Churches in a total Catholic Unity.

What characterizes Caodaism is its spirit of synthesis. That is why its conciliating role can render a great service to religions peace, and thence quite simply to peace.

There is no sectarianism in Caodaism, and also instead of tending toward the opposition of religions among themselves, this new religion constitutes and will constitute more and more a permanent call to good will among the various creeds : religious, mystic, philosophical, or esoteric.

Understanding among all spiritual forces will give the world the best harmony at all levels.

Caodaism, as we shall see, is a religious synthesis which, in spirit and in Truth, tends to harmonize all human beings with the laws of the Cosmic Order.

In order to penetrate the rites of this new, and at the same time, very old religion, it suffices to be spiritually free, intellectually sincere, cordially kind and physically at the service of Good.

The spiritual freedom required is that which relieves the being from dogmatically imposed restraints and mental frauds due to the undemonstrated « a priori », and that in the practice of the Universal Good.

We can say and we shall see it in following the present book, that Caodaism, beside the inspired part, possesses in itself, aside from the « Message », a whole set of propositions, the distinctness and precision of which are a charm to the Reason as well as an evidence for the Intelligence. Whether these reasonable propositions be first of all « messaged » or « inspired », the effect is still that of a mystic progression in the attractive radiance of he Doctrine which tends with all its divine and human force to fundamental Truth, to integral Beauty in the practice of the Universal Good.

What will surprise certain readers is that Caodaism arises from contemporary revelation, and that this revelation is attained through the course of spiritism.

We should rather surprise the conformists who love their readymade ideas, well-ordered classifications, and relationships as logical as they are artificial, if we would reveal the « spiritist sources » of the principal, great human movements from Joan of Arc to Caodaism.

The « spiritist » character of the military genius of Jean of Arc was demonstrated by the work of Lieutenant Colonel, Collet, who published at Nancy, 1920, a « Military Life of Joan of Arc », with technical precision and rational statement, for he is competent to judge concerning inspiration through the luminous analysis of the theories of Spiritism of Gabriel Delanne, Brierre de Boismont, Léon Denis and some others.

That which inspired Joan of Arc also inspired in the Occident one of the greatest poetic, literary, political, esthetic and religious movements which we put under the general term : Romanticism.

In fact, Ossianism, as we know, is one of the roots of European Romanticism. It was engendered by the work of a medium, James Macpherson. It is a case of the so-called « spiritist medium prior to litterature », James Macpherson, who produced in English prose the bardic messages, originally expressed in the Gaelic language by the poet King Ossian, a bard of the 3rd century.

James Macpherson has been accused of literary fraud, because, naturally he had employed the « Gaelic poems » in every document. These message-poems were dictated to him by the spirit of Ossian in the very language of the medium-writer, but in a style and rhythm so original that they forced the enthusiastic admiration of most of the great writers of his age and the following Turgot, Diderot contributed to making these poems known to Europe ; and Mme de Stael considered Ossian as the « Homer of the North ». Chateaubriand did not withhold his admiration even after the accusation of literary fraud. We have these messages (1760-1763) in a French translation by P. Christian (Lavigne, publisher, Paris 1842).

P. Christian is the author of the famous, basic « History of Magic ».

The messages of Ossian were dictated (or inspired, as we like to say) to James Macpherson during a period of three years (1760-1763) : Fingal, in six songs ; Comola, a dramatic poem, the war of Inistoma, the Deliverance of Carrictura, Cathon, Darthula, war of Témora, etc... on the whole, about a score of poems of various lengths.

These poems lost their prestige in the eyes of the public when they were attributed to literary fraud. We have reason to believe that Shakespeare, Walter Scott, and some others were, like James Macpherson and Victor Hugo, the inspired mediums of Romanticism. They transmitted the messages as James Macpherson transmitted from Ossian.

It would be interesting to publish some day « the Spiritual Origins of Romanticism » and Gabriel Gobron brings us to this subject an inspiring and documented source of incontestable originality and authenticity.

What is curious to us is that : it was P. Christian, a man initiated into the occult, and a medium himself, who translates into French the works of Ossian, the 3rd century bard, the Gaelic poems « received » by James Macpherson. P. Christian closes his introduction with these lines, regarding these poems which « maintain » here and there a comparison with those of Homer, and often lean toward Hebraic poetry which has been so much praised, and perhaps so poorly understood ».

The proofs of the spiritist origin of Caodaism will be easier to demonstrate than that of Ossianism ; and it is also to render homage to, and by this means to communicate with the Hereafter, that the present work was published, recast, clarified, and completed.

It is spiritism that led Gabriel Gobron toward Caodaism, as the latter has been revealed by spiritism.

Caodaism is a true, reformed. Buddhism, it is also a particular form of spiritism : the Vietnamese Spiritism.

We add today, in order to make it complete, the synthesis of religions, because what we desire to reveal to the public is revealed in the present edition.

Since Caodaism, born of spiritism, reformed Buddhism, and afterwards expanded into a harmonious synthesis of all religions, it did so without losing the best of its spiritist origins or of its Buddhist formation.

Being true theosophy, the Caodaist doctrine draws to it through perfect selection all that was good, beautiful, and above all essential in the other religions, whether in the practical, the moral, the ritual or in philosophy.

Due to the great modesty of Brother Gago (Gabriel Gobron is so-called by the Caodaists of Indochina), he willingly limited his role to that of polemist-advocate, propagandist of the new religion. His essays, his meditations, his study of mysticism merited more. We can say today that he is the first philosopher and the first historian of Caodaism.

His work seemed to be unfinished when he left the earthly life for the Eternal Orient, but with the publication of the present work, his value as historian of Caodaism is confirmed.

From the Beyond, Brother Gago enlightens and protects us still, for such was the profound will of his faith.

Piously, let us listen to him, accepting his mission with a wholly Caodaist humility.

If we have accepted this ungrateful role of first historian of Caodaism, it is because our brothers and friends of Vietnam have judged in their excessive indulgence that we were one of the best informed Westerners on the progress and tribulations of reformed Buddhism.

Feeble health hardly favors the overwhelming duties of such a charge. We apologize to the attentive reader, for all the imperfections of our work. We ask him only, above all, to pardon us when we cannot stay « in line », that is to say, fraternally, even toward our adversaries and enemies : It is then that the Caodaist will have proved Unworthy. He will not have attained selfmastery. The patient will have torn his cap in a fit of ill-humor, and stamped the most sublime pages of Christ, Buddha and Confucius...

By compunction, we have transmitted the message, It only remains for us to turn over in silence to the reader, relieved of our comments, this posthumous work of Gabriel Gobron.

DELECOURT-GALLOIS.
(Executor of the will of Gabriel Gobron)

HISTORY AND PHILOSOPHY

OF

CAODAISM

THE ORIGINS OF VIETNAMESE SPIRITUALISM

Rev. Stainton Moses undertook a six month's retreat at Mount Athos in which he studied theology, confronting various contradictory theses. An excellent exercise which recalls the spirit, always prone too be doctrinaire, dogmatic, intolerant, to greater humility, wisdom, and truth. He was then named to a little pastorate on the Isle of Man where he never lacked for leisure : Nature, reading, prayer, meditation, silence and mystic contemplation made him a poignant orator : The Imperator *Spirit* had already seized him, and intended never to release him, no more than his demon would release Socrates. Imperator led Rev. Stainton Moses to Oxford University, but above all, made of him one of the most precious instruments of the « New Revelation », one of the most sublimely inspired mediums of our age.

---

(1) The British National Spiritist Association was founded in 1873, partly through the initiative of Rev. Stainton Moses who formed eleven years later the Spiritualist Alliance of London, today the most powerful in England. (page 35, René Sudre, introduction à la Métapsychique humaine, Payot Edition 1926).

Thanks to the help of Stainton Moses and several others, Crookes succeeded in founding on February 20, 1862 the «Society for Psychic Research» (S.P.R.) « which played a considerable role in the history of metaphysics ». (op. cit. page 38).

It was in the same solitude, the same calm meditative retreat, that Cao-Dài found his first Caodaist. No temple more beautiful than that nature, no book more divine than the book of life. Jesus retired to the Garden of Gethsemane, even to the desert ; St. Francis of Assiz spoke to his little sister the rain, to his little brother the wind, to the silent stars, to the talkative swallows, and he stroked the jaws of the wolf of Gubbio and brought it home like a pet dog. The Swedish naturalist Bengt Berg nestled in his hand the the wildest bird of Lapland.

VHERE THE HOLY IS,
THE EARTH IS HOLY.

Where the holy is, nature rises above itself.

The Holy rises in man, It is man above himself.

The Holy rises Within man above the level of mankind in communing with the Spirit.

Thus, on the threshhold of this book, we must listen to the voice, which says :

From the height of the roofless tower where Ecstasy had carried me, I regarded the world, sad and cold, black and shaken.

From the height of the roofless tower where Faith had raised me, I saw afar the sea, guarding its blue quietness like a veiled Virgin.

From the height of the roofless tower where faith had led me, I saw the dawn of an eveless morning and an infinite day.

From the height of the roofless tower where love had placed me, I beheld the sun lighten the earth.

The sad cold world turned red and warm.

Black became white, and white was changed into black. Peace and harmony reigned in the world.

From the height of the roofless tower, my heart wept for joy, my soul saw ecstasy, my body broke with pain.

From the height of the roofless tower, I saw the shadow ship crossing the sea of light, and wondering, I contemplated the Mover of stars, the Ordainer of worlds.

I saw the elements, the seasons, and the months obey the Watcher.

The great and watching Eye.

From the height of the roofless tower, I saw in Him, by Him, for Him.

The First Caodaist

It was early in the year Bính-Dần (1926) that Caodaism was founded. But for six years, one man had been worshipping the Great Master Cao-Dài. Mr. Ngô-văn-Chiêu, who was at that time in the service of the criminal investigation department of the Cochinchina government.

As an administrative delegate in 1919, at a post called Phú-quốc, *an island in the Gulf of Siam*, Mr. Ngô-văn-Chiêu led a life of great wisdom, conforming to the stern rules of Taoism. From time to time, in this isolated place so favorable to the religious life, he gave himself, with the help of young mediums from 12 to 15 years of age, to evoking the great Spirits (Cầu-Tiên) from whom he received the necessary instruction for his spiritual growth. Among the communicating spirits, he discovered one named Cao-Dài, in whom he became particularly interested.

From the first, this name caused general astonishment among those present, for to their knowledge, no religious work had ever made mention of it. Chiêu, nevertheless, whose wisdom was admired by all, by means of his revelations and philosophical studies, believed he recognized a surname of God.

Having asked Cao-Dài for permission to worship him in tangible form, he was ordered to make representation in the form of a symbolic eye.

PRAYER TO THE EYE OF GOD

Eye of God,
Thou art the gold and the crystal of heaven.

Ethereal essence of all essence of all things, Thou seest in all.

Bodyless spirit expressed in a look (the wise never confuse the symbol with that which it represents). Thy vision is infinite.

Total intelligence, penetrating, enveloping : Zodiacal.

Life : Principle of life, life of all principle which the sun's regard develops and multiplies in the Gold of Heaven.

Night's repose in the light of the moon :
Crystal of heaven.
Sidereal light.
Solar light.
Lunar light.
Unique light in the eye of God.
Unique light of the eye of God.
Thou Three-in-One of the One-look.

Eye of God
Bathe my spirit in the light of crystal and gold.

— Amen — »

Such was the conversion of the first Caodaist, to the new religion, that it was able, six years later, to plant itself in Saigon. Soon, Mr. *Chiêu's* administrative duties recalled him to the capital, where he made several proselytes to the new faith. But let us leave for the moment these first converts, to show the reader the manner in which the Great Master recruited his mediums.

It was the middle of the year Ất-Sửu (1925). A little group of Vietnamese secretaries belonging to various branches of the administration a Saigon, amused themselves evenings by dabbling in spiritism. They made use of a « ouidja board ». Their first attempts were mediocre. But through patience and practise, they finally obtained results. Their questions put to the spirit, sometimes in verse, sometimes in prose, received surprising answers. Their dead parents and friends showed themselves to talk of family affairs and give counsel. These sensational revelations taught them of the existence of an occult world.

One of the communicating spirits became particulary noticeabbe by his high level of moral and philosophic teachings. This spirit who signed himself under the pseudonym « AAA », did not wish to reveal himself, in spite of the entreaties of his hearers. Soon, other secretaries came to swell the little group of amateur spiritists, The meetings became more serious and regular. As the ouidja board was no longer convenient, this spirit replaced it by the « corbeille à bec ». With this apparatus, which permitted direct writing, the communications became more rapid and less fatiguing for the apprentice-mediums.

On Christmas eve, the 24th of December, 1925, the guiding spirit, who, until then had obstinately guarded his anonymity, revealed himself at last as the « Supreme Being », coming under the name of Cao-Dài to teach truth to Vietnam. Speaking in Vietnamese, he said in substance :

« Rejoice this day. It is the anniversary of my coming to Europe to teach my doctrine. I am happy to see you, O my disciples full of respect and love to me. This house will have all my blessings. Manifestations of my power will inspire even greater respect and love in my regard... »

From that day forth, the Great Master initiated his disciples in the new doctrine.

Such was the calling of the first mediums charged with the reception of the divine messages.

I asked the Great Master, who from the nearby Beyond made answer.

I asked the Great Master, saying, « Venerated Lord, what is the earth ? »

The Spirit replied :
The earth is a vessel which rocks in an ocean of light.
This light is time and space.
Time is invisible light.
Space is visible light.
Thus time envelops space as spirit envelops all.
Time hovers above, within and without.
Space abides beneath, without and within.
Of invisible space is time
Of the passing of time is space.
The earth is a vessel that rocks, rocks in an ocean of light.
The earth is time condensed. The weighting of spirit in matter.

* *

Consulting the magazine *l'Inde Illustrée*, which undertook a series of articles on various religious manifestations in British India, Siam, China, Japan, the Philippines, etc., we find in N°. 2, dated March, 1933, a study on Caodaism in Vietnam (South). We read concerning its origins :

« Of recent date (1929) Caodaism has growm rapidly and spread through all Cochinchina.

Origin. — Early in 1926, some young Vietnamese scholars, all Buddhists, gathered in a compartment in the middle of Saigon. They had the habit of « table tipping », and giving themselves to spiritist experiments.

After a period of groping about, they finally obtained some « surprising » results, they said, by means of some of their number who possessed a powerful « fluid ».

They were at first in spirit communication with one of the Chinese sage of antiquity, Lý-thái-Bạch, more commnly known as Li-tai-pe, the Chinese Homer, author of a literary revival under the 13th Tang dynasty (713-742), a fervent Taoist.

Thus, once again, we seem justified in our sub-title: Caodaism, or *Vietnamese Spiritism*

A French Testimony

It is that of Mr. Jean Roos, writing in *le Colon français* of Haiphong, on the origin of Caodaism:

1926! The year is just beginning!

In a few days comes the Vietnamese Têt. Not far from the Central Market, in a block of shop-houses of modest appearance, occupied for the most part by employees of the administration and large business firms. In one of them, since many long months, young clerks from Customs, Public Works, the Railroad, and various business houses find themselves from evening to evening playing with the table — tipping it, making it talk. They are all Buddhists. How did it all begin ? One of them had heard of spiritualism, of the most important tables, in his office, where one of the bosses, a Cochinchinese, is a convinced spiritualist, member of one of the most important spiritist societies of France. He, in turn, had spoken of it to friends, and one day, they found themselves, four of them, seated about a table.

« We'll see if this works ! We'll see if there's anything to it ! » they said. The beginnings were not very brilliant, but, little by little, eliminating those who did not possess the «fluid», replacing them by more gifted friends, they marked up extraordinary results. They never failed to receive answers to their questions put to the table. They asked if they were truly in communication with a spirit. The answer was affirmative.

The thing became serious. At each session, they asked the name of the spirit who spoke to them. Most frequently, Lý-thái-Bạch, or Quan-thánh-Đế-Quân, or sometimes a person unknown. Thus, that which, at the beginning, had been only an amusement with a touch of that mysticism which nearly always flourishes in the Vietnamese soul, became a privileged conversation with the superior spirits of the occult world of whom they asked counsel.

No doubts were raised concerning the nature of the conversations, first, because it was equally new to all, it was impossible to suspect one another of connivance, and later, because certain communications from the correspondent of the occult world revealed such lofty sentiments, scientific knowlege, and depth of philosophy that none among them was capable of being the author.

But the use of the tipping table to correspond with the occult world was not very practical ! So much time was required for receiving the shortest sentence !

It was at the time of which I speak, that is, shortly before the Vietnamese Têt of 1926, that they made known their complaint to the spirit.

It answered that they should make use of the corbeille.

And since they asked what that was — (those more or less versed in spiritism or having attended but one seance will see what novices they still were) — the spirit told them to address their compatriot, the Phủ-Chiếu, one very deep in spiritism, for it would be too difficult for himself, to make them understand by means of a table what he was talking about.

Thus, Caodaism was about to be born, or rather was about to enter into the stage of its popularity, since, for many years as we shall see, one man had been worshipping Cao-Dài.

This man who followed the holy doctrine of Gautama Buddha, was none other than the Phủ-Chiếu. Besides the moraltea chings of Buddha and those of Confucius Whom he venerated as emanations of the divine, he believed in the existence of a Supreme Being, All-powerful, Sovereign Master of the Universe, called Cao-Dài. He believed also in the spirits with whom he claimed to have been in relation for years. The dignity of life of this first Caodaist, to whom the young men were sent, was exemplary. His compatriots unanimously considered him a holy man. He taught the clerks the use of the corbeille à bec, to which I shall return later, which greatly facilitated their spiritualistic seances. He participated with them, happy to make use of mediums particulary apt, gifted, and possessed of unusually powerful fluid.

After having entered into relations with the Phủ-Chiêu, it was under the same conditions at the invitation of the same spirit, that they went to find another of their compatriots, a former Cochinchinese mandarin, a member of the governement counsel, Lê-văn-Trung, who was given from time to time to spiritualist seances. Lê-văn-Trung, whose name the young clerks didn't know until the spirit told them, had not always led a life of exemplary wisdom. He had, on the contrary, gotten the most out of life to the point that, at the moment that the young men were sent to him, he had nearly ruined all his fortune.

Having already passed the half-century mark, Lê-văn-Trung who seemed in everyone's eyes an impenitent materialist, in his amateur spiritist hours, considered as a warning from the Supreme Being the fact that he, with the Phủ-Chiêu whom he had long known, had been chosen to show the way to the young spiritists. He resolved from that day to lead an exemplary life and to show himself worthy of the mission to which he had been called by Cao-Dài. He immediately ceased smoking opium without the slightest inconvenience (which proves, say the Caodaists, how much he was strengthened by the Supreme Being, for without help, he could never have cured himself so easily), he abstained from alcohol, from the eating of meat, became, in a word, a sincere Buddhist priest.

This miraculous conversion attracted to him the first group of adherents, in general members of well-to-do families, or well-placed government officials, among which was Phủ-Tương, in the provincial administration of Cholon, who was, like his colleague Chiêu, a man of superior morals, practising on every occasion the humanitarian virtues dear to Confucius, the Đốc-Phủ Lê-bá-Trang the honorary Huyện Nguyễn-ngọc-Thơ and his wife, the former Mrs. Monnier, a very rich Cochinchinese, who had long used a part of his income for works of benevolence and charity.

The Phủ-Chiêu who had first of all been designated to fulfil the functions of supreme Chief of the religion, the pope of Caodaism, decided to retire and was replaced by Lê-văn-Trung.

Upon asking one of the principal dignitaries for the cause of Mr. Chiếu's attitude, I was told that since he had been the first caodaist of Cochinchina, he would normally have been called to fulfil the functions of supreme leader of that religion, but that he had shown himself incapable of overcoming a temptation which God had assigned him as he imposes to all superior beings before raising them, from low degree, to a scale the top of which is perfection and he was, therefore, obliged to redeem this weakness of which he had given proof before taking back the place to which his past seemed to give right.

The Pope of Caodaism

The conversion of Mr. Lê-Văn-Trung who was to become Pope of Caodaism, was one of the great events of Indochina's history.

It was also in 1925, Mr. Lê-Văn-Trung was living in the city of Cholon. Given to diverse enterprises, in the tumult of that town devoted to the worship of money, he had a spirit completely averse to religion. One evening, at the invitation of one of his relatives, a convinced spiritualist belonging to a religious sect called « Minh-lý » at Saigon, he went to a seance that was to take place in the suburb of Chợ-gạo.

At that meeting, it was the spirit Lý-Thái-Bạch that was manifested. Taking Mr. Trung aside, he revealed to him his spiritual origin and at the same time announced to him his future religious mission. He then exhorted him to quickly submit himself to the regime imposed by the new faith. Moved by grace, Mr. Trung without hesitation, sustained by his faith, had the courage to cease smoking opium and follow a vegetarian diet ; he also left his business enterprises in order to consecrate himself entirely to religion.

The conversion of that man, the day before still attached to wealth and pleasure, is so striking that we may ask ourselves whether the spiritualistic seances organized at Chợ-gạo had not been inspired by missionary spirits with the unique aim of bringing back Mr. Lê-văn-Trung in the way of the Law. In fact, when the latter had made up his mind to live according to the new faith which he had adopted, they ordered the dispersion of the spiritualistic group, to the great astonishment and sorrow of its members.

In Saigon, the Great Master, feeling the time had come, united the mediums of Lê-văn-Trung. He then sent two of these (Messrs. Cư and Tắc) to the newly converted, with the order to organize there a seance during which, he should give him instructions.

Mr. Trung although he did not know these mediums, yet accepted their proposition when he understood their motives.

An evocatory seance took place. The Great Master, besides other teachings, announced to Mr. Trung his great mission in the new religion he was going to found to save humanity.

That revelation confirmed the allusions of various spiritualistic messages that Mr. Trung had received at Chợ-gạo with other mediums. It fortified his conviction and encouraged him to consecrate himself without reserve to religious exercise.

Some time after, the Great Master sent Messrs. Trung, Cư and Tắc close to the Phủ-Chiểu, who had to guide them in the religious way as an elder brother. This man having been so ordered by the Great Master, welcomed them most cordially. He immediately put them in contact with his first co-religionists. The caodaist cell thus formed was composed of a dozen members, all of French culture and most employees in various administrative departments in Saigon.

The earnestness and disinterestedness of these pioneers soon attracted to them an increasing number of adherents. The Caodaist religion then came out of its limited circle to spread among the people at the begining of the year Bính-Dần (1926).

The Phủ-Chiểu used to his solitude, was annoyed by the influx of adherents who bothered him. As an official conscious of his responsibilities, he decided from then on to keep himself free of this great religious movement. Mr. Lê-văn-Trung was then named by the Great Master to replace him at the end of April.

First meeting-places

Spiritualistic seances continued more and more numerous at individuals' homes but mainly in meeting-places organized in each of the following centers : The town of Cholon, Cần-giộc, Lộc-giang, Tân-định, Thủ-dú'c and Cầu-kho.

Two mediums were appointed to each place to receive the teachings of the Great Master. The admission of new members was also decided there. Adherents came in mass, amounting to hundreds of new enrollments at each seance.

Official declaration of the Caodaism

The new religion was very rapidly extended, it was received with much enthusiasm, especially by the masses. Anxious to act openly and keep themselves in the strictest limits of legality, its leaders made an official declaration signed by 28 persons, which they sent in on the 7th of October, 1926 to the Governor of Cochinchina. Also enclosed was a list of signatures of 247 members present at the ceremony announcing the official existence of Caodaism.

Propaganda

After having made that declaration which was courteously welcomed by the local Government, the leaders of the « Great Way » organized propaganda missions in the interior.

These were three, one for the provinces of the East, one for those of the Center and one for those of the West.

In less than two months, over twenty thousand persons among which many native notables, were converted to the new religion. It was on account of spiritism, and especially to the infinite kindness of God who was always manifested at each invocatory prayer and whose messages had a decisive influence over spectators, that Caodaism received these mass conversions. The great success was also due to the form of the new worship which had nothing contrary to that of the principal religions practised in the country.

Festival of the Advent of Caodaism

Since the 10th day of the tenth month (October 14th, 1926) the propaganda tours were interrupted. Every effort of the leaders was concentrated on the festival of the advent of Caodaism. This took place on the 14th, 15th and 16th of the tenth month of the year Bính-Dần (November 18, 19, 20, 1926) in the pagoda *Từ - Lâm - Tự*, situated at Gò - Den (Tây - Ninh). The Governor General of Indochina as well as the Governor of Cochinchina and high-placed European and native officials were invited.

Celebrated with solemnity, this festival gathered a considerable number of believers from all the provinces of Cochinchina, It also attracted thousands of curious come simply to observe. The presence of Captain Monnet, a great French spiritualist, was also noticed there.

It was during this festival the Caodaist sacerdocy was instituted and the new religious code was established and promulgated.

Definite see of Caodaism

The *Từ-Lâm-Tự* was a buddhist pagoda newly built by the Hòa-Thượng *Giác-Hải* of Chợ-gạo (Cholon), who had allotted it to the new religion to which he had been converted. But after the festival, the buddhist faithful who had furnished funds for the erection of this temple who had not been consulted on its transfer, demanded its return.

On the other hand, experience had shown that that pagoda was too small and that the land on which it was built was too exiguous to enable them fitly to install the Holy See of the incipient new religion, which promised so great a future.

On indications of a superior Spirit, the land on which the temporary temple is actually placed was then chosen and bought to locate the Caodaist Holy See. Situated at the village of Long-Thành, province of Tây-Ninh, it is large enough (about 100 hectares) to meet with actual and future needs.

The transfer of the Gò-den Temple at Long-Thành took place on March 1927. The number of adherents continued to increase considerably. The movement of pilgrims to the new temporary temple is worthy of notice : it was by thousands that they were received there daily.

As any other religion at the beginning, Caodaism had also its adversaries whose criticism, often too passionate, was not always dictated by a sufficiently objective spirit.

However, the caodaist leaders obeying the instructions of the *Great Master*, endeavored to maintain and improve themselves in the Great Way only considering the moral and spiritual good of humanity. It is the only answer which they are allowed against attacks of which they are the object, for every caodaist keeps his temper.

At last, after four years of existence, Caodaism counted half a million adherents. And in spite of multiplied obstacles sowed in its way, it always continued its triumphant walk towards the goal that God assigned to it : the regeneration of humanity in universal peace.

Sources of the Doctrine of Caodaism

L'Inde Illustrée gives an abridgment of it as follows :

« Cao-Dài is a symbolic name of the Supreme Being who, for the third time, is to be revealed in the Orient. The opinion of the adherents of the new faith is that God, adapting his teaching to the progress of the human spirit, which is more refined than formerly, should this time be manifested by means of mediums, He being unwilling to grant any mortal the privilege of founding Caodaism.

« This new manifestation of the Supreme Being arose from the fact that all religion submitted to the authority of a human founder, is opposed to universality, since its prophets rise up against truths proclaimed by other Religions towards which they show an obvious intolerance.

« The Caodaist Doctrine is a fusion of the oldest religions of the Orient : Buddhism, Taoism and Confucianism.

« In a message transmitted on the 13th of January, 1927, in the presence of several Frenchmen, Lý-thái-Bạch, one of God's ministers, made clear this doctrine. We take from it the following lines :

« The holy doctrines of the various religions are ill-practised. The order and peace of the days of Yore is effaced. The moral law of humanity is betrayed. For unthinking and sceptical persons, God exists in name only. They ignore the fact that in His supreme place reigns a Personage, Sovereign Master of all events of the universe and all human destinies.

« Formerly, the peoples of the world did not know each other and lacked means of transportation. I then founded, at different epochs, five branches of the Great Way (Dại-Dạo).

« 1º Nhơn-Dạo : Confucianism ;
« 2º Thần-Dạo : Khương-Thái-Công, *worships of Genii ;*
« 3º Thánh-Dạo : Christianity ;
« 4º Tiên-Dạo : Taoism ;
« 5º Phật-Dạo : Buddhism.

« Each based on the usages and customs of the races particularly called to practise them.

« Nowadays, all parts of the world are explored : humanity, knowing itself better, aspires to real peace. But because of the very multiplicity of these religions, men do not always live in harmony. That's why I decided to unite all in one to bring them back to primitive unity. What is more, the Holy Doctrines of these religions have been, through the centuries, denatured by the very persons charged with spreading them to such a point that I now have taken the firm resolution to come to you myself to show the true way...

« In that same spiritualistic message of the 13th of January, 1927, Lý-thái-Bạch also said :

« Dear Brethren, the merciful Christ came among you to mark out for you the good way. Try to follow it in order later to have peace of soul ; go forward each day with alert step in the love of God. Unite in love one with another, help one another, this is law divine.

« At that moment, when each is condemned to undergo his purgatory, if he think of his own interests, if he seek to sow misery and suffering, he will risk to be drawn into the infernal torment where the wicked goes to crush his life and soil his soul ».

Indeed, Caodaism or Dại-Dạo is the most simplified religion that exists at present so far as the practises of its worship are concerned ; it merely asks its adherents to address daily prayers to Cao-Dài, either at home, or in appointed places ; no confession (spiritualistic evocations being delicate and dangerous to handle, are reserved to the sacerdocy), nor communications. The number of Priests reduced to strict necessity for preaching from time to time, the holy doctrine, exhort the faithful to practise the virtue of humanity such as Confucius conceived. If it exist but one God, the Supreme Being, it recommends to its members to follow pure christian morals or that of Confucius, which, actually, do not greatly differ.

It recommends the veneration of the Superior Spirits, who were benefactors of humanity at different epochs ; Christ, as well as Buddha Gautama, Confucius and different Genii of the Chinese antiquity, are not forgotten in prayers.

Dignitaries of Caodaism, on principle, are forbidden evocations of spirits before the masses of the faithful in order to avoid becoming professional and abusing the credulity of the mystic crowds. The billed basket is veiled in the temples. But inspired mediums continue to be heard by the faithful. It would seem then, in my opinion, unjust to declare too quickly that the founders of the Caodaist religion put their light under a bushel and reserve to themselves the monopoly of contact with the invisible. It is sufficient for him who practises the religion that he may rise to acquire the right to a more complete initiation. In some respects, it is the attitude of the Catholic Church toward spiritism.

FUNDAMENTAL PRINCIPLES CONFIRMED IN 1946

The Caodaist doctrine tends not only to conciliate all the religious convictions, but also to adapt itself to all degrees of spiritual evolution.

1) *From a moral point of view*, it reminds man of his duties toward himself, his family, society, that is a broadened family, then toward humanity, the universal family.

2) *From a philosophical point of view*, it preaches the despising of honors, riches, luxury, in a word, the emancipation from servitudes of matter, to seek, in spirituality, the full quietude of the soul.

3) *From the point of view of worship*, it recommends the adoration of God, the Father of all, and the veneration of Superior Spirits that constitute the occult August Hierarchy. Admitting the national worship of ancestors, it prohibits however meat offerings as well as the use of votive paper.

4) *From a spiritualistic point of view*, it confirms, in harmony with other religions and systems of spiritualistic and psychic philosophy, the existence of the soul, its survival of the physical body, its evolution by successive reincarnations, the posthumous consequences of human actions ruled by the law of karma.

5) From the initiates point of view, it communicates to those of the adherents who are worthy, revealed teachings that shall enable them, by a process of spiritual evolution, to accede to ecstasies of felicity.

Adherents

They are of three kinds ;

1) *Religious :* high dignitaries who are constrained to lead the life, if not of an ascetic, at least entailing certain privations : the works of the flesh are forbidden to them : they keep their wives, but they are to them no more than sisters ; alcohol, meat, fish, are forbidden to them ; they partake exclusively of vegetables. They are authorized to commune with God and the Superior Spirits, but only occasionally.

2) *Mediums* : to the number of twelve, who are somewhat auxiliary, and are not actually monks, but are yet compelled to certain rules, certain privations in their material life. They continue to take care of their daily occupations, in commerce, or industry. They are formally forbidden to practise spiritism, save in the presence of the dignitaries and with their invitation after having recited prayers to the Most-High.

3) *Ordinary members :* the mass of believers, whose duties are only to follow the morals and rules of behavior indicated by the Directing Committee of Caodaism and especially, to prostrate themselves every day before the altar of Cao-Dài, either in a special pagoda, or in a newly created meeting-place, or at home before the altar which certain have erected, on the throne of which is found the drawing of an eye surrounded with clouds, before ritual candlesticks, a perfume-burner full of ash in which josssticks are burned, and offerings such as fruits in more or less abundance.

According to another more recent document, I find the members divided into two categories :

The *thượng-thừa* (superior degree) and the *hạ-thừa* (inferior degree). In the first degree are all the real monks ; they may be dignitaries or simple adherents. With that title, they are compelled to grow a beard and long hair, to follow a diet of exclusively vegetable food, to abstain from luxury and sexual intercourse. Their life, freed from servitudes of matter, is entirely devoted to the service of religion.

The second degree comprises the mass of the believers who continue to look after their normal occupations ; their religious duty consists in daily practising the worship and observing the rules of conduct prescribed by the new Religious Code (*Tân-Luật*). These as well as the others are forced to « *ngũ-giới-cấm* » (the panchashila), interdictions drawn from the buddhist morals commanding not to kill, to avoid cupidity, luxury, gaiety and sin in words.

Concerning the diet that the members of the second degree must follow, a gradual vegetarianism is prescribed to them, consisting in abstaining from meat a fixed number of days per month.

So they begin with the « *sóc, vọng* », temporary diet of two days ; then successively pass to « *lục trai* », diet of six days ; and to « *thập trai* » diet of ten days.

The Caodaism admits to its fold all men of good will without distinction of race, or social rank. There the simple « *dân* » fraternally rubs elbows with the « *đốc-phủ-sứ* ».

Caodaist Worship

This is practised every day, in places of meeting as in private homes, in four hours (*tứ thời*) : 6 a.m., noon, 6 p.m., and midnight. Prostrated before the divine altar, in the leap of the soul toward the Supreme Being, we begin by fulfilling the rite of the offering of incense (*niệm hương*). Then comes that of the offering of prayers (*khai kinh*), the form of which may be translated as follows :

« Above the ocean of human pain in which immensity is lost between sky and sea, already the Day-Star points to the East.

« Lao-Tze, the Great Teacher had the merit of aiding our human salvation.

The *Three Religions* teach as base of their doctrine the practise of good and of virtue.

« *Confucius the Sage* has clearly traced the path of the *Middle Way.*

« *Buddha the Merciful* preached devotion and charity.

« The Taoist doctrine ordained the worship of truth and character discipline.

« 'Tis thus that one trunk gave birth to three similar branches.

« Let him who can penetrate truth so profound, purify his heart for the recital of holy prayers.

These formalities ended, we entone in chorus a hymn to the glory of God, then three in honor of the *Holy-Three:* Confucius, Laotze, and Buddha.

Such is, in all its simplicity, the daily worship rite. As for the divine services celebrated in the temples on great ceremonial days, we shall observe a more elaborate ritual.

How to pray to Cao-Dài

I ask of you, my Brethren, to pray and sing the praises of Him who gives life, strength, beauty and what is still better: wisdom that makes you like unto him. I ask of you, my brethren, to sing, pray and put yourselves in order.

Position of order standing in the station of montionless waiting... I ask you to await the benefections of the Spirit.

Position of order standing in the gesture of the first step toward the Light... I ask you to walk toward the Light.

Position of order seated in waiting and inner meditation... I ask you to meditate, pray and wait.

I ask you, my Brethren, to pray, inwardly singing the praises of Him who gives life.

The life of the body to run to the help for those who have need of you.

The life of the heart to love all men, all beings, to love all life, all divine life, angelic, human, animal, vegetable, mineral and atomic life. I ask you to love earth, water, fire, air, the pebbles of the road and the stars of the heavens.

Position of order in repose. That of rest which must be an action of grace.

Immobility is an order, a position of action, a prayer, a song toward Him who gives Life, Strength, Beauty and what is more, Wisdom.

My Brethren, My Sisters, I ask you to pray and sing the praises of Him who gives life.

I bring flowers of five colors. I bring flowers.

The white lily of innocence, candid, united with God.

As all colors are found in the white of the faith, so all beliefs are of one.

The blue of the fields of heavenly hope. The blue of the heavens which induces the upward look.

In divine hope are all human ideals.

The red rose of bleeding love, of love crucified, the red rose of charity.

The rose that carries the cross.

The cross that carries the rose.

Rose-Cross.

The yellow sun-flower, the gold sun-flower, the sun-flower of silent speech.

The gold of heaven falls on the earth.

The mauve flower, the violet of secret humilities. The violet made of red love and blue hope. The violet of morning, but also of secret power.

The mauve color of him who knows truth.

Universal Love

Those simple words might sum up the essential tendency of Caodaism.

The practical applications that come from it concern :

1) *Human brotherhood* ;

2) *Kindnes toward animals.*

« For we are entrusted with duties of fraternity toward men who are our brothers in the universal family, we also have duties of goodness toward animals who also are our brethren behind us in the way of evolution. We must then take care of those destined to our service, treat them with gentleness and avoid making them suffer needlessly. All animal life must be respected as much as possible : for in harming it, we delay the evolution of the victim. So all caodaists conscious of their duties will submit to a vegetarian diet to avoid being party to multiple crimes daily committed to the prejudice of his inferior brethren.

« Between pity toward beasts and kindness of soul », said Schopenhauer, « there is a close link: we may say without hesitating, that when an individual is cruel toward beasts, *he will not be a just man.*

3) *Goodne toward plants :*

« Nobody is ignorant of the services rendered us by all kinds of trees. Silent benefactors of man, not blaming either his ungratefulness, or his cruelty, they shelter, with their shade, all who come and sit at their feet, a tired traveller as well as a wicked woodpharmacy cutter. The sandal-wood, it is said, perfumes the axe that strikes it.

« Plans constitute a true natural pharmacy from whence is drawn all proper panacea to heal every desease. How many lessons of goodness and sacrifice can we draw from it for our profit !

« The recent scientific experiments of Sir Bose, a scholar of India, have shown that plants live much like man, that some, particularly sensitive ones, possess a nervous system more sensitive than ours to physical impressions. What think we then of him who amuses himself by chopping a branch from a tree or uprooting a plant ? If the necessities of material life oblige us to use vegetables, the goodness we owe these « candidates for animality » recommends us never to mutilate, nor needlessly destroy them.

4) *Service to one's neighbour* (that completes the duty of the human fraternity).

« What sweetness, what charm, nature in its solitude, offers him who lives the quiet, secluded life. Apart from the world whose temptations attract him no more in the quietness of his seclusion, he purifies his life, calms his passions and raises his thoughts toward the Supreme Being. Then, in the rapture of contemplation, where is revealed the feeling of Divinity, he feels at last his heavenly origin.

« Such is the inner life led by Superior Men endowed with great faculties when, their terrestrial mission fulfilled, they aspire to spiritual well-being. But before reaching that high stage of human pilgrimage, the traveller of the long road, while seeking to progress, must help those who feel their way behind him.

« So the caodaist, anxious to act according to his principles of humanity, must, in every circumstance, devote himself to the service of his neighbour. Impelled by a desire to help his fellowmen, he holds himself in readiness to bring, either by his words, or by his acts, a balm to moral and social miseries. And, in his aspiration toward merciful love, he always holds out the same helpful hand to those who stand in need. Bearing all affronts, from whatever source, he remains without hatred among them who hate him, ever faithful to the *Great Way*, dignitary or simple believer, he must impose upon himself the difficult task of working for souls, to instill into them the teachings of Cao-Dài, based on the love of good and the worship of truth. If by dint of proclaiming truth, he does not succeed in convincing unbelievers, at least he will shake them a little. Until doubts subsided in their souls, time will accomplish the rest.

« It is in setting himself to the help and salvation of others that he works for his own, for the acts of love and charity, by a just return, constitute his only viaticum in his wanderings toward supreme happiness. Since the service of one's neighbour is one of the indispensable conditions of his own salvation, it is in his interest to apply himself to it with as much zeal as his religious earnestness and his moral advancement enable him. Without pretending to place himself as a preacher, he must, however, particularly incite his coreligionists to the practise of good and virtue. He can reach it, not by vain speeches, but by practising what he preaches and conforming his life to the doctrine he professes. If at times he fails in that task by slipping from the way that was traced for him by the Great Master, it is but just that we blame his weakness or his backsliding and not the teachings which he is charged to spread which constitute — may we repeat ? — an ideal of peace by fraternal love.

There may be, in Caodaism as well as in all other existing religions, hypocrites and believers whose faith is not strong enough to resist the temptations of the Spirit of Evil. These are the unhealthy elements that dishonor the religion to which they belong, and of which the body must be purged.

What Caodaism Brings

Caodaism comes to unveil truth and confirm the goal of the creation of man.

Caodaism gives to its followers a consciousness of his power when the spirit is united with the Spirit.

Cao-Dài comes toward man hindered in his walk toward the light and shows him that human reason will triumph over all obstacles, all misunderstandings.

Cao-Dài delivers from hinderances.

Caodaism is then in harmony with the free man who freely believes that the human spirit will one day be conscious of its own power.

But Cao-Dài guards the free man from the spirit of pride, for he says that all inner light comes from the superior light.
Light comes only from light.
The Light here below proceeds from the light above.
Human light proceeds from divine light.

Predestination of Caodaism

Caodaism is predestined to become not only in the Far-East but in all the universe, a synthesis of religions, a supertheosophy freed from artificial theosophy. Caodaism does not seek for religious transcendence, but hopes for and tends toward a harmony of beliefs and philosophies. None of its principles may be refused by any even somewhat advanced mind.

As in all epochs, there was a way opened toward the Light from above, just as in every place is found erected a mystic or material temple to invite the blessing of the Cause of causes and to try to elevate microcosmic man toward the macrocosmic all.

Religions everywhere, in all times, the living religions of to-day: hinduism, buddhism, judaism, christianity, and islamism, are adapted and adapt one another to the time and place of their formation and development. It is aquatic environment that gives a fish its form. It is the attraction of Heaven that makes man walk erect.

Caodaism, born in Indochina, is destined for the universe, since the message it brings is found already in all religion.

The multiplicity of religions is not an obstacle to harmony if a subtile but real bond forms a point of contact for them, That link, Caodaism brings to him who will listen without prejudice, with all sincerity, fraternity, to its message : Life, Love, Truth.

Caodaism, Religion and Philosophy

Caodaism is a valuable religion that unites its members one with another, that unites the incarnate of this time, in all places, with the disincarnate of the past and that prepares for future reincarnations. Caodaism makes its own the comtist formula: «*The dead necessarily and more and more govern the living.*» But, for it, the dead are really and always living.

The caodaist doctrine is a valuable philosophy that is set forth, demonstrated, discussed and affirmed with sincerity, with rationalism as well as in mysticism. Rationalism is not necessarily a systematic atheism.»

There is only one God, what is his Name ?

There is only one God, first Cause, principle of all that exists. There is one God worshipped, venerated, prayed to under diverse names at every point of the globe. There is only one God.

Cao-Dài, such is the name that the one and total God has taken to manifest himself in Vietnam and to indicate to the world the new religion in which men are certain to find Him.

Cao-Dài, such is the name of the unique God who is in all the present and past names man gave to God or under which God manifested himself to man.

Cao-Dài, such is the name.

Cao-Dài

Cao-Dài is the most high Palace. It is the manifestation of the Ensoph in Kether.

Cao-Dài is a roofless tower on the platform of which is written « He that man cannot name » by any human words. Ensoph of the Cabalists, Iod, He, Van, He of the Israelites.

Cao-Dài serves as the name of God. It is one of numerous names of the One-God whose name can only be one of the aspects, while the Being is infinite.

By the triple-sign, the tri-um God is always shown on the summits. God is higher than any summit, broader than any space, more enduring than all time.

TAM = Let us worship three times God-One in Cao-Dài.

KỲ = God is eternal in all time and at all time. The present moment is always His time, the epoch of God.

Cao-Dài manifests Himself in the three periods of the past, present and future.

PHỒ = sacrifice, fast, anticipation, prefiguration of that which is to come, of that which is come. The fast is an expectation of celestial food, the divine Word. All holy men and wise feed on the Word. Thus the sage, as the monk, expects through fasting and abstinence from what is terrestrial to feed on what is celestial.

In the fast thou shalt find Cao-Dài.

ĐỘ = Thus cometh deliverance as shall come the resurrection.

Thus cometh judgment and pardon.

So is manifested *Cao-Dài* to pardon and to love.

Tam - kỳ Phồ - độ
QUAN - ÂM BỒ - TÁT

Secret feminity of a mysterious Goddess who gives strength to God.

God is One and the Goddess contains Him.

She is One and all God is manifested in Her.

Quan - Âm Bồ - Tát.

SECRET DIVINITY, tabernacle of God and God-Thyself in thy feminine expression.

Quan - Âm Bồ - Tát
manifests herself in
Cao-Dài
as Mary at Golgotha.

Golgotha = bald mount = roofless tower. On the heights God is manifested.

Five interdictions

1) *Not to kill living beings* (because of the spark of life, the center of consciousness that is in them).

2) *Not to covet* (in order to avoid the fall into materialism through the needs of possession and domination). Such is the case of existing society in which everything seems bound to stir up pride and the craving for riches.

3) *Not to practise high living :*

— Don't eat the bodies of beasts (vegetarianism) ;

— Don't drink alcohol (because of its noxious effects on the physical body and the spirit).

Noxious effects of alcohol on the perispirit :

« The perispirit, said we, interpenetrates the physical body and envelopes it in its fluids. Its vital center is in the brain and its astral center, on the fontanelle (1). *(It is on the latter center that the Spiritual Protector (Hộ-Pháp) remains posted to watch over the Ego of an ascete till the day when he reaches complete initiation).*

« Now, the exciting effect of alcohol, which spreads to the brain, congesting it, provoking troubles in the perispirit, troubles which, to the great prejudice of the ascetic life, destroy the mystic harmony that is established in the believer. Moreover, during those perispiritual afflictions, he leaves the door open (the astral center) to perverse Spirits who, taking possession of his body and exercising their control over him, impel him to reprehensible acts that may lead him to perdition.

« Therefore our Great Master has expressly forbidden us to drink alcohol ».

4) *No to be tempted by luxury* (which attracts a cruel karma) ;

5) *Not to sin by word :*

---

(1) *Nê-huờn-cung in Vietnamese : Brahma-randhra in Sanscrit.*

« Revelation teaches us that God appoints a guardian-angel to the care of each human life. That spirit, with a rigid impartiality, is, by virtue of his mission, ceaselessly in relation with the perfect Beings of Superior Hierarchies to render, before the Counsel of Lords of Karma (Tòa Phán-Xét) an account as full as possible of all our good or ill deeds. Therefore the account of all human acts, constituted in merits and demerits, is unavoidably settled by the Great Karmic Law. Further, that Spirit appointed to our care also has a mission to teach us from his inspirations. Men, in their poor and insufficient language, call him *conscience*. Now, before we seek to deceive others by our lies, we must already have deceived our conscience, that is to say our guardian-angel. He records not only all our actions, but also our words, though they be not yet expressed in acts. For, to the eyes of the Lords of Karma, the sins of the tongue, as sins, are as punishable as those arising from an overt fact.

« So must we observe the greatest circumspection in our speech as in our acts ».

Creation of the World

The creation of the world is always real and this religious truth is propagated from century to century according to the times, in harmony or against opposition. The creation of the human spirit is always actual and its elevation is constant. He who does not evolve, involutes and falls again into matter.

The spirit is materialized, incarnate to live among us, but returns to the Spirit, training and purifying us by him. Many messengers of the Spirit have come : Krishna, Shakyamuni, Confucius. Elsewhere : Hermes and Pythagoras, Socrates and Plato.

All the messengers have had their disciples : The Essenes, the Gnostics, the Templars, the Rosecrucians and a great many others in the Occident and in the Orient. Nowadays, in the Far-East : the Caodaists.

French spiritualistic messages

Those who are received most frequently by the Caodaist mediums emanate, it is said, from Allan Kardec, Léon Denis, Camille Flammarion, Descartes, Joan of Arc, Chateaubriand, etc... *and especially Victor Hugo and the Hugo family.* Several leaders of Caodaism, the Vietnamese pretend, are but the reincarnation of several Hugos. Several curious facts seem to make it believable. In certain temples, is placed the portrait of Victor Hugo.

Reincarnation in Caodaism

Being connected with buddhism, taoism, confucianism, and I think I may affirm without fear or successful contradiction : with kardecism (Allan Kardec being considered as a religious genius), Caodaism believes in Karma, and Samara, its consequence. The caodaists frankly declare to bring nothing new on that point.

All volition (thought, word, or act) is a *cause* that bears in it its *effect* :

« The cause is rigorously bound to its effects, which is somehow its transformation, its material interpretation. That interpretation is so exact that the scrutiny of the present incarnation of an entity should be sufficient to inform us at the same time of its past and future. The present incarnation of the entity with that alternation of joys and annoyances was determined by the actions that it had fulfilled itself in the course of its anterior lives. Likewise, from now on, its deeds determine the conditions of its future reincarnation.

« The effect is separated from the cause by a time thay may be long or short. If that interval is short, the effect is immediate and the sinner sees the expiation accomplished before his eyes. If it is long, it is because the sinner is benefitting for a time from the happy effect of good deeds accomplished at some time in the past, and that still lasts. But as soon as that metapsychic immunization is ended, the karmic law will have full play. In many cases, the fall incident to it is sudden, thus explaining the quick decadence of such and such a family, a dynasty or a race » (*Revue Caodaïste*, March, 1933).

The free-will of man is limited by the karmic effects of the anterior lives, man being the real artisan of his own destiny, affirm the Caodaists. The practise of good enables the entity to get rid progressively of its karma. « To know himself, said Ngô-Văn-Chiêu, the first Caodaist, lately disincarnated, the believer must wish himself unhappinesses. »

Caodaism also believes in the apparition of a *new man*, thus uniting either with Professor Pietro Ubaldi *(Zeitschrift fur metapsychische Forschung)*, April 29th, 1933), who believes that man in the future will be a natural medium, a new type of sensitive being, or with our friends the theosophists, who already perceive the new type of man in formation.

« Experience has shown that at each coming of the Messiah, whether He bears the name of Laotze, Buddha, or Christ, humanity is as it were awakened from its torpor. A stream of occult forces circulating everywhere helps him to understand mysteries heretofore incomprehensible ; a sudden and marvellous development of such faculties as intuition, memory, intelligence, clairvoyance, empowers the believers to accede to the way that is now open. Touched by the universal fluid, which comes near the Earth only after thousands of centuries, the faithful easily understands the divine teachings and, blazing the trail, some day he will succeed in being absorbed in God.

« Since the appearance of Caodaism, whose founder is the Supreme Being, phenomena of that kind were noticed somewhat everywhere in Cochinchina. The most surprising is the integral vegetarianism practised without trouble by the members of all sexes and ages. We have seen many children of four or five, who could not bear a dish of fish or meat. We have seen many aged 13 or 14 years, renounce a meat diet to eat vegetables and rice once a day. We have seen others who ate only fruits. These facts of a new order astonished the bonzes themselves, who confessed that even among them very few practise a true vegetarianism.

« Then comes the unexpected expansion of certain faculties such as memory, intelligence, intuition among persons who have received no instruction. »

Since its creation the « Revue Caodaiste » has drawn our attention to some cases of reincarnation in Vietnam. We should be very happy to see our caodaist brethren adopt for their inquiries and control the scientific precision necessary to the Occident which wants proof more than witness of a moral nature. They would render us an immense service on that point : One case of minutely controlled reincarnation would subdue at a stroke the objections current and a hundred times heard against reincarnation. The « Revue Caodaïste » has already undertaken such and we congratulate them upon it.

Each of us, says Caodaism, before being reincarnated, takes a little cháo-lú (soup of forgetting). If he takes much (when he has many sins and he has much to forget), he does not remember his previous life. If he takes a little (when he reaches one of his last reincarnations and he needs no longer blush at grievious faults), he is able by introspection, intuition, and illumination, to remember incidents of preceding incarnations. But it is the privilege of an elite of humble and silent meditative men and sages whom the world ignores.

∴

Our era of failure, chaos, hate, thirst for riches, speaks readily of tax reform, treaty revision, frontier changes, revision of customs duties, etc... But it forgets a reform which is little spoken of, but which is the key to reform of all reforms.

Are we beginning to reform our conscience ?

It is because Caodaism understood this necessity and attempted that reform of conscience that so many black forces in Asia are raised against it. Powerful synthesis of the Asiatic religions ; a link with the christianity of Christ ; a rallying of psychic and spiritualistic fact, basis of modern occidental spiritualism ; a cry of love toward the Unknown, the Infinite, the Universal Peace and the Fraternity of peoples ; greetings to thee, Cao-Dài, greetings to you, caodaists, distant brethren of Vietnam, which we now receive and bless in precept and example. Does at last old Europe dare overthrow those values that necessitate the advent of a new day ? We believe so, and therefore we say *thanks* ! to our caodaist brethren of Indochina.

CAODAISM AND VICTOR HUGO

Religio, the *Rivista di Studi Religiosi* under the direction of Ernest Buonainti, in Rome, has also consecrated an article to Caodaism. Mr. G. Mingiano writes (p. 478) :

Victor Hugo and the Caodaists : — One of my friends who is travelling in the Far-East, writes me from Saigon : « Do you know that Victor Hugo has been deified ? It is by a sect of Cochinchina, called Đại-Đạo-Tam-Kỳ-Phổ-Độ, that has had the strange dea to attribute to the great French poet divine honours. What do you think about it ? While in France a referendum was called to find the worthiest manner of celebrating the fiftieth anniversary of Victor Hugo, with ceremonies proceeding at the Pantheon, at the Sorbonne, at Guernesey, all kept in the strict banality of official honours, here is a religious sect of Cochinchina which confers on the Poet divine honours and inscribes his name in the Legion of the Genii. So a man was called to honours of the altar (or almost), that, in his famous will, denied all value and religious content to constituted churches and accepted only the prayer of the humble.

Let us give to the gesture of the Caodaists its true proportion : the glorification of human genius understood as an expression of the divine light ; the glorification of Poetry, understood as a human expression of the divine harmony. A form of glorification that is naturally framed in the fundamental conceptions of that new religious confession which, in less than ten years of life, has been able to gather nearly a million adherents.

I knew in Paris, toward the end of 1931, a student from Phnom-Penh, who was in attendance at the Sorbonne. He was a caodaist. I learned from him that the Đại-Đạo-Tam-Kỳ-Phổ Độ, — which means precisely Caodaism — was founded in November 1925 and represents a synthesis of the three great Oriental religions : buddhism, confucianism and taoism, which united with christianity and the worship of genii, represent the five great ways that Cao-Dài (the Supreme Being) opened to humanity for their development and spiritual evolution. As we see Islam does not find place among the ways that lead to the Most-High. Christ, on the contrary, is considered by the caodaists as an Envoy of the Lord to a part of humanity, to guide them along the way to perfection, a way adequate to their capacity for understanding spiritual values.

The sense of profound veneration with which the young Indochinese student pronounced the name of Christ, the respect with which he told me christian rites of which he knew the occult signification, were for me, I confess, the highest, the most efficacious lesson of tolerance, at the same time an example of true fraternity in a Superior Being, who, in spite of the diversity of names with which men invoke him, changes not at all His face of shining love.

« What does it matter, really, whether a spirit be actually that of Fénelon or not ? If he speaks nothing but good, and talks like Fénelon himself, he is a good Spirit ; the name by which he is made known is of minor importance, and often is only a means of fixing our ideas ».

Allan Kardec
Cited by René Sudre

« Know that all have known His law, His end, His way ; that stars and distances all hear Him ; that all is conscious in creation ; and that the ear can have His vision ; for things and beings have their dialogue ».

What the Shadow's Mouth said. »
Victor Hugo, Jersey, 1855

Victor Hugo was during his lifetime a practising spiritualist, he communicated by means of a table and automatic writing. His desire while living was that he might appear to his friends after death. Therefore the Hugo messages are more easily « authenticated » than those of a Fénelon (to cite the example of Allan Kardec) or of any others.

Moreover, the solemnity of the message that I am going to reproduce here, the eminent quality of the interpellator, postulate in favour of authenticity.

Here is then the spiritualistic message attributed to the Spirit of Victor Hugo or Nguyệt-Tâm Chơn-Nhơn, in the seance of the 20th of April, 1930, at 1 o'clock in the morning.

Hộ-Pháp : *I wish to be instructed regarding the origin of our Master and his Power.*

It is not easy to know this mystery,
The eternal searching of the question is not clear.
It is possible there are, in my opinion,
Other universes than ours in the infinite.
They would be more or less enormous,
But life and their beings would have the same form.
One of these would be more advanced.
From the point of view of spirits and humanity.
At one stage, they should much resemble ours,
With progress they could become apostles.
In all the heavens, Beauty reigns,
Its beings possess much of divinity.
Peace and harmony rule these earths,
Their creatures know not the word « War ».
Nothing is relative, all is absolute ;
Great souls vie with each other in virtue.
All production is science and wisdom.
Soul-power is master of human weakness.
These latter worlds live without law,
Union is made under faith divine.
Death will be vanquished by uplifted conscience.
There is no difference between living and dead.
The love of all beings is published everywhere,
Souls and men are all in holiness.

There is, here, a certain world of ours,
Where this kind of life is fruitful.
You may, one day, appreciate its value,
Then our world has passed to the higher degree.

Hộ-Pháp: *When will the earth have these benefits:*

In order that you may be conscious of your merit,
I will make use of a spirit expression.
Through purgatories, beginning at the rank of the blessed,
The land will be long becoming the land of the gods.
If one would know the origin of our Master,
He must be with him so as to penetrate it.
No spirit has a clear opinion,
Buddha himself only suppositions.
Do not take my instructions as important.
I only repeat what the spirits think.
Let us suppose that the creator, in his beginnings,
In reality lived in one of these universes,
His sipirit also had to make a long ascent;
From matter, He became man, then a sage,
He passed through the grades of the spirit class;
And entered at last into the mystery of Creation.
Through his successive lives, He possesses a power,
That has made Him Master of Wisdom and Science;
He surrounds Himself with the best of the spirits;
Which make up His court of servants and friends.
As soon as His heaven had power enough,
He rode with His train through infinity.

Hộ-Pháp: *He has, then, a heaven of his own?*

Yes, each of us has a domain set apart.
That He makes with his spiritual force.
Souls and spirits that proceed from our karmic state,
Thus form our heaven and make our republic.
Those who people it are scarcely faithful,
Many among us come from our original sin.
To the extent that one neglects the secrets of purification
He opens the heavens to these terrible demons,
From which comes our Satan, the great devil.
If we search for the truth and not fables,

He surely comes from the cortege divine
Which our Creator was unable to make perfectly holy.
It is the rule that our nearest betray us,
Through jealousy, envy, or pure caprice.
You have, Hộ-Pháp, a cramp in your hand,
Let us put off our talk till to-morrow.
I continue my discussion of Genesis,
Respecting that which will please you.
Once on a time in a shadowy place,
Still, stagnant, peaceful, unmoving,
In a gas neither vapor nor liquid,
Slept sommolent germs and lethargic ;
Envelopped at last in a frightful cold,
No creature lived, no matter germinated.

Hộ-Pháp : *Is this the nature of the water spoken of in the christian Genesis ?*

Yes, it is this form of gas which is called hydrogen,
More or less dense, which makes the purest part.
Say that the Spirit of God swam above the waters.
It is in this sense that the word must be understood.
With its star made up of light,
It animates by its heat inert matter.
A layer of oxygen is produced, goes into action.
The contact of gases makes an explosion ;
Divine fire is born, and holy water is formed,
Under the effect of the two elements, all is transformed.
From burned matter was formed gas, from burned gas
Were produced fluids, pure fluids are vitality.
Such vitality has a power
Of giving the spirits both death and life.
What marvels are already shown us ?
What mysteries are further reserved for us ?
All that comes from the hand of our Master,
It is difficult for us to know.
This divinely fed fire, expanded,
Casts its nebuli afar to the infinite.
In all the universe this fire is sown.
It is renewed as quickly as decomposed.
These nebuli grow in the form of suns ;
Creating worlds in all their details,

Which the consciousness of God and His light animate,
And the weakest of beings have penetrated all.
The spirit divine is everywhere spread.
All that have life proceed from this All.
Of the fluids emanating from the light divine,
The most impure are changed into stone,
Into earth, into vegetables, animals and flesh.
The most dense into air, and the pure to ether.
Intellect is thus given to all creatures.
According to their state, a dose more or less pure.
Soul is thus created, as for the body
'Tis vitality that determines its lot.

    The rest you have understood
    I stop here.

Hộ-Pháp : *Pardon, if all comes from our Master, all must be perfect. Why then do we observe imperfection in nature ?*

What are these imperfections ?
May I give you some explanations ?

Hộ-Pháp : *The wickedness and uselessness of beings, as well as men, animals, and vegetables. Their morals cannot be reasonably appreciated,*

Nothing is wicked or useless in nature.
To be preserved, there must be nourishment.
The Good Lord ardently loves His children,
In His great love, He finds them the means.
For their progress, He creates for them suffering.
They must also have means of defence.
Have you seen in this world a man truly pious ?
Though they be wicked to us, they are useful to them !
How did our great sages become so ?
What do the pages of human history contain ?
A fierce struggle between the weak and the strong,
The strongest are often the greatest.
The opposition of the two gives the upward march
Of ideas and wise realizations.
Our dear world is purely relative ;
Wicked and useless are only qualifications.

On the globe, each of us has a place;
The worlds of other heavens are but classes.
The universe is therefore a school for the spirits.
Who attend it for erudite study.
Those who fail in their efforts,
Must repeat the same classes, and study their lessons again.
All spirits hope to read the eternal book
That holds the secret that can make them immortal.
The goal is achieving our rude career ;
Which takes time, conditions, and manners.
From the material world to divinity pure
Is eternity's road to be taken.
The result is learning self-knowing.
And then knowing, through conscience, the man that should be.
The difference in characters is right ;
'Tis an aid in making comparisons.
Make romm for great tolerance in your studies.
Class the spirits according to their aptitude.
Simply separate those who are human
From those already a little divine.
Give to the leaders the best example,
Teach by all methods the unfaithful,
Do not detest them for their infamy
And think only of the salvation of their souls !
Love always in order to give to humanity
These two verities : Love and Eternity.

Hộ-Pháp : *The Father and the Master are different. Why does our Father take also the title of Master,*

He is at the same time Father and Master,
For from Him comes all of our being.
He nourishes our bodies with that which is good
And makes up our spirit of what is divine.
In Him all is science and wisdom ;
Progress of soul is his unceasing work,
Vile materials are jewels in His eyes
Vile spirits, He makes into Gods.
His law is love, His power is justice.
He knows but the virtue, and none of the vice.
Father : He gives to His children vitality.
Master : He bestows on them His own divinity.

WHAT ARE THE CAODAISTS ?

In *Religio, la Ravista di Studi Religiosi*, Mr. G. Mingiano writes :

« The caodaists are divided into two categories » The first one comprises all the ecclesiasts, from the « pontife maximum » to the last novice, all bound to a severe diet of chastity, poverty and frugality, (They live exclusively on vegetables and fruits) rigorously observed. The hierarchy is on an initiatic basis and comprises seven grades of initiation : The highest, that of « eldest brethren », has the exclusive privilege to communicate with the « messengers of God », high spirits of light from whom they receive energy, teaching and counsel.

« In the second category, is all the mass of the faithful, which, besides buddhist duties, must observe humility, honesty, respect of authority, wherever found, and at last, obedience to religious authorities. Worship consists only in common prayers to which the faithful are convoked before an altar, on which is placed a great transparent sphere containing the sacred fire. On the sphere, a triangle, symbol of perfection and composition of divine energies in the triangle, the earnest eye of the Eternal ;

« In this religion, two aspects are, it seems to me, most original :

« The first is this : To become a caodaist, one needs make no profession of faith, he need not be bound to any sacrament : freedom of conscience is sovereign. The institution lives and prospers, not of the forced will of its adherents, but of their free consent, their spontaneous and voluntary adhesion. As a result, no anathema greets or follows him who decides to try another way. The prayer of all, on the contrary, renders his new effort easier. And that, because the caodaists not only recognize, but feel that the terrestrial life, the life in time and space, is a trial, a test, an experiment, that each one must realize in order to make a step forward on the way of Cao-Dài, the Most-High. And each one has the right to choose his way. The search for riches, the conquest and extension of material power, are condemned by the caodaists, because for them too, the « kingdom of God is not of this world ». But it is at the same time a duty and a right to gain economic solidarity and to be able to give moral and material assistance. This is the source of the second original aspect of caodaism : From the civil point of view or rather for its social action, caodaism has special institutions in crafts, teaching, outside relations agriculture. etc... to intensify its work of social welfare, coordinated and efficacious. »

The review *Religio* follows this article of Mr. G. Mingiano with these lines : « Oriental wisdom, that marvellously shields it ».

« Pai-Te-Tien was a Chinese poet. Being governor of a district, he paid a visit to a sage, a great disciple of the ZEN sect, who had chosen his dwelling in the branches of the tree. Pai seeing him, cried : « What a perilous dwelling is this tree ! » To which the sage replied : « Yours is much more perilous than mine ». Then follows this dialogue :

« I am governor of the district. I don't see what risk I am running ! »

« Then, you don't know yourself ! What peril greater than the passions that burn you and your troubled spirit ? »

« What is the teaching of buddhism ? »

« Don't do evil ; practise good ! But that, a child of three years knows. Yes, a child of three years knows it, but an old man of 80 years such as I succeeds with difficulty in applying it. »

« Han-Shan, a poet, was a pure fool, who came to the monastery Kuoch'ing to gather the left-overs of meals and feed on them. The monks laughed at him as a poor, innocent and harmless fool. One day, in his hermitage, Han-Shan exclaimed : « I think of all those past years during which I quietly came to Kuoch'ing, where everybody seeing me said : « Han-Shan is a fool ». At present, I think : Am I foolish ? I don't succeed in solving the problem, not knowing myself. And then, how can others understand me better than myself ? »

« Be man not fond of talk, in order to find God in the silence. Pray, the heart full of desire, but without uttering a word. God shall provide thee with thy needs and hear thy voice, and welcome thy offering. As well as in a desert the water of which is so sweet to him who burns with thirst, divinity is shut to him who speaks, open to him who keeps silence. »

Message of Wisdom

You kill one another, disputing the hills, the rivers, the lands, and the seas. You kill each other for possession of that which was created by the One in Three, the Three in One, though you are His children, and He is Creator of all.

Ambitious, selfish, wicked, you close your purses, and in them shut up your hearts. How will you love one another, for the love of the One in Three, the Three in One ?

>To preach peace, there must be love for all men.
>To practise concord, pardon of all to all.
>What is the highest nobleness ?
>What is the highest superiority ?
>What is the highest origin ?
>All men are sons of God. So God was called : the Son of Man.

You knock at the door of wisdom. A voice demands :
Who is there ?
You answer : It is I. And the door opens not.
You knock at the door of wisdom, a voice demands :
Who is there ?
And you answer again : I. Do not be astonished if the door does not open.
You knock at the door of wisdom, a voice demands :
Who is there ?
You hesitate but answer : Thou. At last, the door opens, and you enter into wisdom.

CAODAISM AT THE INTERNATIONAL CONGRESSES

We were charged by the Holy See of Tây-Ninh (South Vietnam) to represent Caodaism at various International Congresses :
1º *International Spiritualistic Congress of Barcelona* (1934) We read in the *Revue Spirite d'Octobre* 1934 (p. 505), in the series of resolutions adopted unanimously.

« *Eighth Caodaist Movement*. — On the motion of Mr. Gabriel Gobron, instructor in France of Caodaism (or Reformed Buddhism, or Vietnamese spiritism), the 5th International Spiritualistic Congress held at Barcelona (1st to 10th of September, 1934) very respectfully begs the French Government to be willing - remembering the solemn promises made in March 1933 in the French Parliament by President Sarraut, then Minister for the Colonies - to establish on behalf of the Caodaists a statute as liberal as that enjoyed by the Vietnamese converted to christianity or those remaining faithful to other buddhist sects in the countries of the Indochina Union. »

2º *World Congress of Religions, London* (1936). *Le Cygne* (September 20 th, 1936) publishes this echo :

« At the last International Congress of Religions held in London, to which Mr. Gabriel Gobron, instructor of Caodaism in France, participated on invitation of the Holy See of Tây-Ninh,

Caodaism is recognized as the most tolerant religion in the world. Before a large attendance composed of representatives of all the Great World Religions and members of the International Press, the French Caodaist delegate declared : « Caodaism is the very experience of the reconciliation of races and peoples for which you are gathered in this place. Caodaism or Reformed Buddhism is certainly a living experience of union and religious unity. Wild applause greeted the peroration. »

3º *International Spiritualistic Congress of Glasgow* (1937). *L'Annam Nouveau* (November 14th, 1937) published this echo :

« At the proposal of Mr. Gabriel Gobron, instructor in France of Caodaism or Vietnamese Spiritualism, the 6th International Spiritualistic Congress meeting in Glasgow (Sept. 3, 1937), after the fifth Spiritualistic Congress of Barcelona, hopes that *the Vietnamese Spiritualists may enjoy in all the countries of the Indochinese Union the same liberties of conscience and worship as protestant and catholic Vietnamese, be they subjects, protégés, Eurasians or foreigners.*

« The wish expressed by the International Spiritualistic Congress of Barcelona has already inaugurated a more liberal period for the Caodaists or Vietnamese Spiritualists. »

That wish presented and discussed in the Philosophical Section of the Congress, was then adopted by acclamation at the popular meeting held at Mc Lellan Galleries on the 9th of September, 1937.

4º *World Congress of Beliefs in Paris* (1939).

Let us extract this testimony from the *Revue Spirite* (Paris Sept. 8) :

« The « World Congress of Faiths » which was formerly held in London, Oxford, Cambridge, took place this year in Paris, our colleague Gabriel Gobron was delegated by the Caodaists or Reformed Buddhists of Indochina to attend it. The rebukes he invoked on the Congress of London may be related here and even enlarged : The organizers, almost all English, address themselves to the historic Religions, which by their long history proved their fecundity (the very words of Mr. Lacombe, Sept. 10, 1939) and then exclude new religions, new doctrines, and still more, syncretic religions such as Caodaism : a close fusion of buddhist, christian, taoist, confucianist and mohammedan beliefs, etc... It is useless to say that spiritism, theosophy, anthroposophy, etc... are banished from that Congress which only seeks the collaboration of the respectable great religions, and never their close fusion or their synthesis. No comparison of superiority of religions was tolerated. The Catholic Church, though officially absent, was in fact well represented (Professor Maritain, Mr. Lacombe. etc...) and it constantly received homage. A hundred persons, many of them Anglo-saxons, officers, administrators, professors, aristocrats, high-bourgeoisie-attended the « days », catholic, jewish, buddhist, protestant, mohammedan, hindu, even interrupting the discussions sometimes outside of the agenda : « How to make the fraternal spirit reign over the world through the concourse of religions ? »

The *official* support given to the Congress (Messrs. Champetier de Ribes and Georges Mandel), its reception in the Sorbonne by the Rector Roussy, with participation of French colonials (one General of the House of the Bey of Tunis, one Syrian Administrator, etc...), of a somewhat gaudy « French Committee », added to the prestige of those solemn sessions at the Richelieu amphitheatre on the 2nd of July, 1939.

« The best of the Congress — in spite of narrow limitations fixed by itself and legitimate reserve — was its will to claim the rights of the individual, now so mocked in all the totalitarian regimes. A resolution recalling the dictators to greater humanity was moreover adopted at the end of the Congress, and the question of refugees seems bound to be inscribed in the order of the day at the next Congress which will be held in Holland.

« A call was issued to all the official Churches. Visits to Versailles, the Paris museums, to intellectual centres, and the mosque where the very Parisian personality, Kadour Ben Ghabrit, courteously welcomed the delegates, etc... followed the daily sittings. They talked too much, certainly, but they also acted :

such a congress is an act, and bears a date. It should be proclaimed more important than the League of Nations, after one of those teas that gathered the members on certain days and revived the flame of the proselytes of the religious idea. »

La Vérité, of Phnom-Penh, seat of the Foreign Mission of Caodaism, expresses it in almost the same language (July 26, 1939) :

Caodaism at the Congress of Religions in Paris (pp. 1 and 5).

« Caodaism or Reformed Buddhism was represented this year at the Congress of Religions in Paris (July 3-11) by Mr. Gabriel Gobron, instructor in France of Caodaism, who again found the leading personalities he had known in London in 1936 ; Sir Francis Younghusband, president, and Mr. Arthur Jackman, secretary.

« The French Government had decided to give its support to the Congress of Religions, in the person of Mr. Georges Mandel, Minister of Colonies, Mr. Champetier de Ribes, Minister of Pensions, the Rector of the University of Paris, Dr. Roussy, who offered the broad Richelieu amphitheatre, in Sorbonne, for the sessions of the Congress. A French Committee, under the chairmanship of Professor Louis Massignon, and composed of various personalities : Mme de Coral-Rémusat, Mr. Jean Herbert, Mme de Margerie, the Princess A. Murat, R. de Traz, Mr. O. Lacombe, Professor Daniel Rops, etc... led the debates, which dwelt on the fundamental theme : How to develop the spirit of fraternal cooperation in the world by religion ?

« Round this problem thus posed, we nevertheless notice catholic, protestant, hindu, mohammedan, buddhist, jewish « days », according to the body to which the main speaker belonged. So, Tuesday, July 4th was a « catholic day ». The Catholic Church officially abstained from participating in the work of the Congress, but, actually, Professor Jacques Maritain, Mr. O. Lacombe, and other catholics played a part of first importance in the Congress week. The church was invisible, but present.

« True, the scope of the Congress was not so great, so universal as one might wish. This was due to certain limitations imposed upon the delegates.

a) No religion must make proselytes by showing its superiority over other beliefs ;

b) It was not to be a matter of union, a fusion of religions, but only of collaboration with different religions while remaining separate ; a religion of union, of synthesis, such as Caodaism, is thus not at ease in such a Congress. So, our instructor in France could declare to Mr. Oliver Lacombe, vice-president of the French Committee, that he was the only « heretic » present ;

c) Access to the Congress, theorically, was reserved to the great historic Religions having proved their fecundity by their long past » (speech of Mr. O. Lacombe, July 1st, 1939).

« Sir Francis Younghusband decided, however, to welcome Mr. Gabriel Gobron, according him full liberty of speech and discussion, after his presentation of official papers from Caodaist authorities at the secretariat in the Sorbonne.

« Mr. Georges Mandel, Minister for the Colonies, had assured the participation of elements of the French Empire in the work and debates. It was thus that General Hasan Husny Abdelwahab, of the House of the Bey of Tunis, an attaché of the High Commissioner for Syria, for instance, represented Islam. On the contrary, our instructor in France does not seem to have met representatives of the French elements of Asia, hinduism and buddhism being represented only by English elements : Bhik Khu Thittila (monastery of Rangoon), Professor Dasgupta (Calcutta) etc...

« Each day, in Paris as in London, in 1936, was composed of an exposé in the morning, then a discussion in the afternoon, followed by visits to places of interest (Versailles, Museums, etc...) and to the Intellectual circles of Paris (Institut de Civilisation Indienne, Mosquée, Association France-Grande-Bretagne, etc...). Our instructor in France having criticized the organization of the Congress of London where isolated intellectuals, representing only themselves (and sometimes their little vanities) he now held the floor for an hour or two, insisting that preference be granted in Paris to *representatives of the communities*, according to the very terms of the rules of the Congress at the Sorbonne. So dilettanti and amateurs found themselves set aside to the advantage of great names like Professor Jacques Martiani (Catholic Institute of Paris), Professor Dasgupta (Hinduism), Doctor Sié (University of Nankin), General Hasan Husny Abdelwahab (House of the Bey), Viscount Samuel (ex High Commissioner for Palestine), Bhik Khu Thittila (Monastery of Rangoon), Professor Hauter (Protestant Faculty of Strasbourg), etc...

« Tuesday the 11th marked an end to the most fraternal and curteous of work and debates. The delegates separated with pain, with a certain wrencht after having passed motions, resolutions, examined projects, improvements, fixed the place of the next Congress in Holland, etc...

« Let us note, among numerous interesting things, a resolution asking Dictators to rule their peoples with greater humanity ; congratulations to Chamberlain for his work of peace ; thanks to French Authorities whose friendliness to all religions needs no further demonstration ; the possibility was considered of Strasbourg, Jerusalem, Geneva, etc... welcoming the next congress ; an invitation to all churches to give the widest publicity to the work of the Congress, of which one orator said that it might henceforth replace the League of Nations torpedoed by politicians and their manipulators. The question of refugees was proposed for the following year.

« The French Committee decided to continue in Paris the work of rapprochement and mutual understanding between the great beliefs... Several inter-religious associations were noted in the capital and offered themselves to delegates desirous of attending their meetings and joining their efforts.

We think that the time is not far off when Caodaism will have to play an important role, by its living example, in these world Congress of Religions ».

5) In 1948

As we have seen, Caodaism is a religion, a body of doctrine, a living tradition, a philosophy, in a word, a spirituality.

Brother Gago was a good prophet, the International Congresses will answer the call of higher entities, but not without difficulty.

Mr. Henry Regnault presented the first edition of the present work to the delegates to the 3rd Congress of the Worldwide Spiritual Counsel, gathered at Lausanne (Switzerland) in August, 1948.

« *None of the delegates knew Caodaism. All were interested to learn that Caodaism has for its ideal the uniting of all religions and bringing of peace here below, which we also pursue* ».

Mr. Henry Regnault was charged by the Congress to enter into relations with the Chiefs of Caodaism asking them to join to the Worldwide Spiritual Counsel.

The answer was favorable and no doubt in 1949, in Italy, Caodaism will be represented to its credit.

***

The spiritual impulse of His Holiness Phạm-Công-Tắc, Superior of Caodaism, is considerable and his radiance oversteps the already broad frontiers of the Far-East to show itself real and growing even in Europe and the two Americas.

POPES OF CAODAISM

Le Populaire (Saigon, November 18th, 1935) published this news : At Tây-Ninh, Mr. Phạm-Công-Tắc succeeds Mr. Lê-văn-Trung as Caodaist Pope.

"On the occasion of the anniversary of the death of Mr. Lê-văn-Trung, Caodaist Pope, grandiose ceremonies took place at the Tây-Ninh Temple, on the 8th, 9th, and 10th of last November, in which more than five thousand faithful participated.

A Great Council composed of Hội - Nhơn - Sanh (popular counsel) an Hội-Thánh (sacerdotal counsel) was held on the 11th and 12th of November at the end of the festivals to resolve the thorny question of the succession of M. Lê-văn-Trung.

Unanimously, the Hội-Nhơn-Sanh and the Hội-Thánh entrusted this difficult task to the Hộ-Pháp Phạm-Công-Tắc. All motions of confidence also obtained a unanimous vote of the Great Council. So was settled a question that has so many times attracted the attention of public opinion.

Let us hope that under the protection of the new chief, Caodaism may quietly go its way.

The newspaper noted the ceremonies : "On the occasion of the anniversary of the death of Mr. Lê-văn-Trung, Caodaist Pope, important ceremonies will take place on the 8th, 9th, 10th and 11th of November at the Caodaist Temple at Tây-Ninh.

Here is the program of the ceremonies :

November 8th. — 2 p.m. : Great ceremonies marking the end of mourning at the Giáo-Tông-Đường.

November 9th. — 7 p.m. Transfer of the Linh-Vị to the Temple ; 8 p.m. Ceremonies at the Temple.

November 10th — 7 p.m. Transfer of the Linh-Vị to the Place of Universal Brotherhood.

November — 6 a.m. Ceremonies before the Cửu-Trùng-Thiên. Funeral orations pronounced by High Dignataries.

« On the occasion of the 10th anniversary, *la Presse Indochinoise* (Sept. 3rd, 1936) reminded the Indochinese public of what Caodaism or Reformed Buddhism is.

« The Caodaism, new religion born in Indochina in 1926, lavished upon the first initiates, by the voice of the Supreme Master, Cao-Dài, its teachings under the form of occult messages that mediums have scrupulously selected to transmit to them for posterity.

« The interpreter of spiritism enables numerous messages emanating from Great Sages of Antiquity, to come regularly from the Beyond to the Holy See of Tây-Ninh (Cochinchina).

The adherents of Caodaism, ever more and more numerous learn that the basis of dogmas is the Law of the Three Saints : Buddha, Laotze, Confucius. The genenal precepts of Buddhism are not to kill, not to steal, not to desire a neighbour's wife, not to bear false witness, not to be drunken. Buddhism goes far in the search for perfection when it teaches love toward one's enemy, a precept that our Occident, which has given the most afflicting spectacle of hatred cruelty, and revenge that history records, looks upon with derision.

First Caodaist Pope,
His Holiness Lê-văn-Trung,
religious name, Thượng-Trung-Nhựt
(disincarnated in 1934).

First Caodaist Lady-Cardinal,
Her Eminency Lâm-thị-Thanh,
religious name, Sister Hương-Thanh
(disincarnated in 1937).

His Holiness Phạm-Công-Tắc
Superior of Caodaism.

Mural : The three Saints, signatories of the 3rd alliance between God and Mankind. — From left to right : Sun-Yat-Sen, called in Vietnamese Tôn-Trung-Sơn or Tôn-Sơn (1868-1925) ; — Victor Hugo, called Đức Chưởng-Đạo Nguyệt-Tâm Chơn-Nhơn (Superintendent of Monasteries) (1802-1885) ; — Nguyễn-bỉnh-Khiêm, commonly called Trạng-Trình by the Vietnamese, first poet-laureate and man of letters of Vietnam (1490-1580), Master of Bạch-Vân-Động (White Stanza).

The mural shows Sun-Yat-Sen holding an inkpot (symbol of Chinese civilization allied to Christian civilization, giving birth to Caodaist Doctrine), while Victor Hugo and Trạng-Trình are writing the words « God and Humanity » (Caodaist Cult), Love and Justice (law and rule of doctrine), the first in French and the second in Chinese characters.

Taoism, of which the doctrine entirely derives from the Revered Book of Supreme Reason and Virtue, develops parallel to its philosophy eminently christian thoughts though it be nearly six hundred years anterior to christianity. It prescribes the worship of truth and discipline of character. This shows that we may meet in the nations considered as barbarous by our ancient Europe, the practise of maxims of gentleness and altruism tending to the maintenance of union and benevolence among men.

Confucianism whose precepts are in no way contrary to our modern scientific spirit, shows a constant anxiety to lift humanity above bestiality by developping qualities, creating a moral and intellectual elite to guide toward happiness the incapable and ignorant who lack the primordial elements of Intelligence, Reason and Knowledge.

To the dogmas of the Three-Saints are added the religion of love and kindness of Christ, the respect of the dead and the worship of the family.

In short, Caodaism gives proof of a great tolerance toward all the existing religions for it includes all, devotes itself to *combat heresy ; sows among the peoples a love of good and of God's creatures, the practise of virtue ; love of justice and resignation ; reveals to human beings the posthumous consequence of their acts, at the same time cleansing their souls.*

Numerous papers announced the manifestations : « Great Caodaist Festival to the memory of Pope Lê-văn-Trung ».

« The Caodaist Temple of Tây-Ninh is very animated these days. Thousands of faithful feverishly work to finish preparations destined worthily to celebrate the memory of the dead.

« The ceremonies that begin on Thursday November 26, at 7 p.m., will last three days. It will celebrate, on the same occasion, the freedom of worship which the liberality of the French Government has granted it. All the Caodaists parishes of Indochina are called upon to participate in the grand program which includes: torchlight parade, and fireworks.

« A Great Festival in view ».

We have been assured that this will be the greatest festival since the foundation of Caodaism.

La Vérité (November 20, 1936) gave an account of the joyful events in these terms : « At the Caodaist Holy See twenty thousand faithful celebrated the 10th anniversary of that religion. Mourning for Pope Lê-văn-Trung is ended.

(From our special correspondent, November 28th)

From all corners ot Cochinchina, Cambodia and even certain Moi tribes, thousands of faithful come to the Caodaist Holy See at Tây-Ninh these days to celebrate the « Đại Tường », after which, mourning for Pope Lê-văn-Trung will be ended.

Exactly two years ago the Caodaist Pope — to use an expression of honour here — passed away. The Caodaist schism is going to be definitely consummated on the occasion of the nomination of his successor.When in the Holy Land the leadership prudently called Monseigneur Phạm-Công-Tắc to the functions of a temporary Chief *without giving him the official title* of the Religion. at Mỹtho, Mr. Nguyễn-ngọc-Tương got himself granted the title Giáo-Tông (Caodaist Pope) by a few hundred followers. The new Pope so named, accompanied by a crowd of partisans, presented himself at the Temple of Tây-Ninh to take up his duties and also assist at the funeral of the Great Departed. Entrance to the Holy See of the new Religion was forbidden to the Chief of the Mỹtho sect, for it is only on « Holy Land » that the true divine speech may come to superiors of the religion by a medium interpreter. Cao-Dài hasn't named His Eminence Phạm-Công-Tắc to the dignity of Supreme Chief of the Religion.

It is understandable that the Caodaist leaders are giving to the Festival of Đại-Tường an unaccustomed splendor. Flower-decked floats would have paraded in the town of Tây-Ninh except for the refusal of the Chief of the province. We feel this refusal to be unjustified since all was carried on calmly enough. Flowery floats, torchlight procession, fireworks during three days of festival increased the popular joy. Electric lights in plenty gave to the Holy Land the aspect of an agitated little city.

We met the high Chieftains. The real Chief of the Religion, whom we had met elsewhere, before his Caodaist conversion, had worked in the customs ; while our childhood friend, Lê-Thế-Vinh, chief of protocol, has been militant in the « Young Vietnam » movement for the betterment of the lot of the Vietnamese people.

This evening, mourning for Pope Lê-văn-Trung will be lifted, speeches read, which will inform us of the movement, its tendencies, its possibilities, its future. We know that Caodaism was born only in 1926, under the impulse of turning tables, imported from France. But what the public doesn't know is that a half-caste Frenchman, faithful reader of Léon Denis and Allan Kardec, has paid with his own money for the propaganda of spiritualistic ideas in the colony, which has contributed much to the extraordinary development of the new religion which puts on the same rank : Confucius, Laotze, Shakyamuni and Jesus Christ. That strange syncretism furthermore explains the rapid success of the movement among Vietnamese and even Cambodians.

The Government might fear for a moment this tardy birth of religion in the very middle of the 20th century ; but since, our leaders have authorized its propaganda in Tonkin ; Caodaist Missions have spread even to France and China.

May not the present manifestation at Tây-Ninh be used as a point of departure for the consolidation and extension of the movement, which has slackened in recent years ?

The Caodaist Chiefs are ambitious to become spiritual Chiefs of a part of the Far-East thanks to Caodaist development.

The near future will furnish us with the key of these enigmas.

Srok Sarou

*
* *

More and more, Caodaism tends to unity. Unity between other religions and itself, internal unity, magnificent harmony around His Holiness Phạm-Công-Tắc who is one of the first followers chosen and named by the Divine Master Cao-Dài and one of the founders of the religion. His Holiness Phạm-Công-Tắc is the Chief, appointed inspirer of the Hiệp-Thiên-Đài, Superior Assembly of mediums. This is a kind of Holy-Office for the proclamation and conservation of the pure doctrine and also cares for the legislative organization of the Religion.

His Holiness Phạm-Công-Tắc was proclaimed Superior of Caodaism by the Popular Council and by the Sacerdotal Council to replace the late temporary Pope, Mr. Lê-văn-Trung disincarnated in 1934.

His Holiness Phạm-Công-Tắc is an inspired man, highly mystic, and as generally is true of mystics, a great administrator and organizer. He is a remarkable builder, for it is he who drew the plans of the Caodaist Temple of the Holy See of which the present work gives several photographic reproductions. He drew up the plans and personally saw to, point by point, all the details of the building and decoration, which is magnificent.

.•.

His Holiness Phạm-Công-Tắc's right hand is His Excellency Trần-Quang-Vinh, Secretary of State for National Defense in the provisional Central Government of Vietnam, since the first of June 1948.

His Eminence Trần-Quang-Vinh has been a Caodaist dignitary since 1927. He has ascended the hierarchic echelons : Lễ-Sanh, Giáo-Hữu, Giáo-Sư, then Phối-Sư, He was Chief of the Foreign Mission of Caodaism. With that title, he resided in Cambodia from 1927 to 1941. From 1942 to 1948, he was a representative of the Superior of Caodaism, residing in Saigon.

Founder, organizer and Commander-in-Chief of the Caodaist Troops.

In 1931, he was sent to France and it was at that time that he created a cell of French Dignitaries and followers among which Gabriel Gobron, brother Gago and his wife, Mrs. Marguerite G. Gobron who may be adressed for information regarding the Caodaist religion in France.

INAUGURATION OF THE CAODAIST
TEMPLE OF PHNOM-PENH

On Saturday May 22nd, 1937, took place that imposing ceremony of which a speech of the Giáo-Su' Thượng-vinh-Thanh, Chief Assistant of the Foreign Mission of Caodaism or Reformed Buddhism (who is believed to be the reincarnation of François Hugo), constitutes the masterpiece. Here are some broad extracts :

« When our hierarchy named me to give a speech to-day when we are going to inaugurate our first church built in the capital of the Khmer Kingdom, I long hesitated to accept this mark of honour, fearing not to be equal to the mission which seemed to me too difficult and too delicate. The insistence of all my brethren of the Sacerdotal Council was required in particular that of our Dean the Bishop Thượng-bảy-Thanh, who is at the same time our Venerable and first Worker of the Foreign Mission of Caodaism or Reformed Buddhism, to make up my mind to appear to-day before so impressive and select an audience.

Speaking a still uncertain French and especially not being used to the platform, I beg all your indulgence toward me.

Please believe, ladies and gentlemen, that you are in a house where peace and concord reign, where the broadest tolerance has the right to be, where the least discordant word must not be uttered, where all they who here are gathered recognize their duty to love one another as brethren and sisters in order to follow the unique law of God the Creator, Father of all, to whatever race we belong, from whatever country we come.

We chose for the inauguration of our first temple the date of the anniversary of the disincarnation of the Great Frenchman, of Great Human, Victor Hugo, who has been since 1927 our much loved and venerated spiritual Leader. We would then show our gratitude to France, the country where the Great Poet was born, that we have learned how to love on the benches of French schools, this chivalrous, generous and humanitarian France.

It was in 1927 that the Superior of the Reformed Buddhism, Mr. Phạm-công-Tắc came to Cambodia and the Spirit of Victor Hugo was first manifested by turning tables, then by the planchettes, at last by a billed basket. So was founded the Caodaist Foreign Mission and the Spirit Victor Hugo became our Spiritual Chief. Under his teachings, we could propagate the new Holy Doctrine, first of all in the territory of Cambodia, then in France and Laos, afterwards in Annam and Tonkin. Let us pay homage to those who frequently took steps in France or in Indochina to defend the cause of Caodaism : Mr. Roger Lascaux, attorney, Mr. Lortat Jacob, attorney, President Albert Sarraut, the Residents Superior Richome, Silvestre, Thibaudeau, the deputies H. Gernut, Marius Moutet, E. Outrey, Paul Ramadier, Marc Rucart, Jean Piot, J. M. Renaitour, M. Voirin, A. Philip, Mlle Marthe Williams, Colonel Alexis Métois, Félicien Challaye, M. E. Tozza, Gabriel Abadie de Lestrac, Jean Laffray (Director of *La Griffe)*, Ch. Bellan, Ex Resident of France in Cambodia, etc. etc. We beg your pardon for any unwitting omission that we might make in this hurried account.

Now here we are gathered in this solemnity for the inauguration of our « House of God » (Domus Dei) at Phnom-Penh.

It is long since at Phú-Quốc, an island situated in the Gulf of Siam, the Spirit breathed as he had already breathed on the Island of Jersey, facing the infinite mystery of the human conscience and destiny, by those immortal tables of Mme de Girardin et de Victor Hugo. It is already long when the Spirit breathed in small family groups in Saigon and quickly brought the adherence of Mr. Lê-văn-Trung who was to become the Venerated Superior of Caodaism or Reformed Buddhism (3rd Amnesty of God in the Orient). Since 1919, but especially since 1925, our movement has not ceased to be confirmed and to win new consciences and souls on every point of the earth.

Certainly, it has met — like all novelties of this world — scepticism, mockery, suspicion, and its most expressive symbols: the Eye of God that is found in a crowd of theologies and philosophies, the swastika that is the origin of all symbolisms and esoterisms of earthly civilizations, the most respectable of our symbols, were held up to ridicule or earned us groundless accusations, because of the ignorance and incomprehension of wordlings who looked only on the outside.

Now, says an old French proverb: « if you would root up the weeds, first go into the garden ».

But it is especially the psychic basis, and why should we fear to call a cat a cat and Rollet a thief, according to the immortal verse of Boileau ? It is especially the spiritualistic basis of our movement that was the object of the easiest and most obstinate jokes. We will not here make an apology for modern spiritism. In spite of ceaseless attacks of which it is the object especially since the last three quarters of the century, the spiritualistic fact did not cease to win famous scholars such as Sir Oliver Lodge, a physicist of world renown, Rector of the University of Birmingham, member of the Royal Academy of England, to take only one example. It did not cease to win islands such as Porto-Rico and Cuba, (the most spiritualistic country proportionately to its population and where the radio carries regular broadcasts of a spiritualistic character), whole countries like Brazil, the « Home of the Gospel » where 8 million inhabitants are acknowledged spiritualists (200.000 in Rio-de-Janeiro); it did not cease to win even universities — unbelievable fact — for Utrecht, Leyde, Belgrade, Lund, Buenos-Ayres, London, several American Institutions already have their chairs of experimental spiritualism. At last it does not cease to be sympathetic with the original thought of our epoch for after having inconstestably decided the prophetic character of the mission and work of Victor Hugo, it has influenced the researches of the three-times doctor Hans Driesch, professor at the University of Leipzig, German theorician of neo-vitalism and the brilliant essays of Allan Kardec and even Bergson. So many things we might add in defence of the spiritualistic fact! But suffice it to say that it is most often ignorance when it isn't prejudice that causes painful human misunderstanding. It is a poor cause, says British wisdom, that cannot keep a smile for the superficial critic.

Furthermore we have veiled the billed basket, recognizing by the example of the Catholic Church, and of enlightened spiritualists, that spiritualistic practises, if they can be, and effectively in all points of the world (there are spiritualistic groups in the ices of Alaska, in the ranchos of the Argentine pampas, in the luxuriant nature of India), starting point of a new birth of man : its spiritual birth, they can also lead imprudent naive persons, individuals with moral blemish, to disastrous results. Saint Paul had already recommended to his disciples the discerning of spirits. And thus it was that the Anglican Church, deserted by millions of its faithful, united by a certain number of its priests spiritualistic associations to consolidate the faith by proof, religion by science, to associate itself in the new direction that humanity demands : (one adult out of seven still frequents the Church in England).

But what is the very characteristic of Caodaism or Reformed Buddhism, is not so much that experimental, psychic basis, that communion of the souls of the living and dead, that glorious and moving fraternity of visible and invisible worlds, as the effort of a powerful doctrinal synthesis we have realized by mixing the Gods of Asia with the Gods of Europe. No « House of God » is in effect comparable to ours, for European or Asiatic, believer or unbeliever may lift up his soul toward his hope of predilection by worshipping Jesus Christ, by venerating Gautama Buddha, or (after the example of free-thinkers of the Occident) by admiring Confucius. That spiritual synthesis tells us where you may find it now, in this world divided by matter, excited by hatred, blood-stained by war. Is there a place where one may, better than in Caodaist temple, work for that fraternity of men, that friendship of races, that solidarity of continents in a wide human gathering having inscribed on its labarum these two words, light of all men of good will : *Spirit, Peace ?* For we dare say, facing the Occident : *We are for Peace.*

Peace with the temporal authorities and chiefs, who also have their mission, often unpleasant and difficult to fulfil in the unleashing of contradictory passions of men. Peace with neighbouring nations, peace with foreign peoples, because war bears in itself so many harms not to be a barbarous superstition or a satanic crime, and the French motto of collective peace, the invisible peace, the peace by conciliation, remains our formula despite the dark hour. Such is the meaning of our spiritualistic synthesis.

It is true that from Europe comes the slight reproach that Caodaism should have excluded from its temples Mahomet and Islam. On our part, there was no ostracism. And it is sufficient to recall here one of the teachings of Mahometan mysticism to see that no Caodaist should refuse to recognize that in this anecdote of *soufism*, the very history of his own birth in the divine manner, his *metanoia* or upsetting of the values of the religious soul.

One disciple presents himself at the door of the master and knocks. Silence. He knocks again. A voice from inside :

— Who is there ?

— It is I.

Silence. The door is not opened.

Later, the disciple presents himself again at the door of the master and knocks. A voice from inside :

— Who is there ?

— It is Thou !

And the door is opened this time.

Truly, a religion that knew how to propagate such truths of a universal nature, a religion that has put upon the lips of certain of its disciples those marvellous words : « I am neither Mahomedan, nor Christian, nor Jew, I am Ouali (God's friend), indeed, I say that religion could not have been the object on our part of any plot, any conspiracy. Let the Mahomedans of India, the natives of the French Mahomedanism believe us in this and recover confidence for our mutual good. And since we have uttered the name of Mahomedan France which has erected its mosque in Paris where five times a day blares from the top of the minaret the call of the muezzin, now it is sweet to us to thank, with all our hearts, sincerely and gratefully Caodaist France, that France which, with its measured spirit, its harmonious will, its fraternal hand always stretched toward the little ones who have not yet realized themselves, has enabled us to be what we are, will help us to become what we shall be. To that France which understood that the 3rd Amnesty of God in the Orient, with psychic and then scientific basis, might reach the universal by the synthetic character of religions which it unites and epitomizes in a daily, peaceful and active fraternity, to that France which encouraged and favoured a new hope in the world, which was recently greeted not only by periodicals such as *La nature* of Paris, but also *Religion* of Rome and *Reformator* of Rio de Janeiro, to that France always ready to exalt and glorify the spiritual and universal, constructive and benevolent values, Caodaism or Reformed Buddhism, from its Superior and its Hierarchy to the humblest of its faithful, now sends the heart-felt expression of its infinite gratitude. In working for our spiritual synthesis, working in the sense of the universal, we are conscious of having worked as Frenchmen, to come much nearer to the French soul with which we believe ourselves to have so many secret and mysterious affinities, that the communion of the living and dead can but strengthen and prove itself in the future.

It is before that joyful fact that we dare to express our dearest desire in the world: That liberal, generous France helps us to spread the benefit of our endeavour to all its subjects and protégés without distinction, for to the thirst of souls spiritual possibilities must be equal to all. Therein is equity, therein is justice. That all may be realized to the maximum and that all may go to everybody working for that edification of the divine, the castle of the soul according to the beautiful words of Saint Theresa in the local and ephemeral man that the wheel of life temporarily ties to the destiny of those « earths of Heaven » where our globe is but a stone thrown among billions of others in the Infinite...

Before those infinite perspectives, what are the stingy limitations that sadly delay the growth of souls whose wakening awaits a ray of light, a flash of fire, so we believe that France shall have perfect confidence in us and give to us the same facilities as to other spiritual powers to invite to our rich feast of divine food, so many of our brethren who may not yet come to us or to whom we may not yet go.

Let France, faithful to its most sublime traditions, be thanked in advance for « service of its neighbour » which is the first and greatest duty of any Caodaist.

This ceremony found multiple echoes in the Indochinese press.

La Presse Indochinoise (4, 22nd, 1937) tells us of a visit to the Caodaist temple at Phnom-Penh:

« The Caodaist temple of Phnom-Penh is situated almost at the corner of Pasquier Boulevard and Verdun Street. — Formerly — eight years ago — it was only a simple straw hut where lived the first missionaries.

After praiseworthy endeavours of remarkable propaganda, the Caodaists at PhnomPenh have attracted into their ranks more than 20.000 faithful, men and women, among which we count several Europeans and one thousand Chinese.

Thanks to the sacrifice and good will of all the believers the temple has at present become a magnificent building. Its inauguration shall take place on the 21st, 22nd and 23rd of next May ; on the same occasion, the festival of the anniversary of father Victor Hugo will also be celebrated. The ceremonies of these two united festivals promise to be splendid. The great chiefs of Caodaism of TâyNinh such as His Holiness Phạm-công-Tắc, Mme Huyện-Sây, will be present at the festivals.

Mr. Đặng-trung-Chữ, chief of the Caodaists of PhnomPenh, with whom we had an appointment to-day at the temple, could not receive us. Urgently called to Châu-Đốc, he was replaced by Mr. Hương who served us as a guide during our visit of the newly built temple. A thin man with an oval face, a high forehead, a little black scanty beard clinging to the chin, Mr. Hương physically represents the caodaist-type. Very enterprising, he guided us through the temple recently done up like new, and with competence gave us all the desired explanations. At the entrance of the temple, a large photo of Victor Hugo, in his classic position of a thinker, at once strikes the sight. Near him on the same table, stands Doctor Sun Yat Sen, the father of the Chinese Revolution. One represents the reformer of Caodaism, the other the propagandist par excellence. At the center, the sanctuary is at the same time austere and soberly arranged. Without superfluous decorations, there is only a paperglobe, an eye painted on cloth then, by hierarchic order, are settled the statues of Buddha, Christ, and the angels.

On our right, « Quan-công Hầu » with a bright red face is reading ; on our left, « Phật Quan-âm » is saying prayers. At the bottom, opposite the Sanctuary, hanging on the wall is a big picture in marble on which figure the names of Moutet, Guernut, Albert Sarraut, Félicien Challaye, etc.

Beside the usual functions of religion, the Caodaists also take care of the education of their children.

We paid a visit to a class led by a young teacher having under his care twenty pupils who, with an admirable cadence, recited aloud the lessons they had learned by heart. All are children of Caodaists, said Mr. Hưo'ng to us not without satisfaction, on accompanying us toward the exit.

On leaving the temple and our guide, we carried with us the impression that the leaders of Caodaism at PhnomPenh have done much for the triumph of their religion ; the results already obtained are the best proofs of their tireless work which will surely be crowned with success at the next inauguration of the temple.

L'Opinion (5, 24th, 1937) in these terms relates the inauguraton :

« According to the prepared program, the Caodaist temple of Phnom-Penh was inaugurated on Friday by various ceremonies to which we shall return later, lacking space to-day for a detailed account.

Here is, however, the text of the speech pronounced by His Eminency Thưo'ng-chư-Thanh, Chief of the Foreign Mission of Caodaism in the course of the first day :

I am grateful to you for coming in such numbers to attend the inauguration of the first Caodaist temple in Cambodia as well as the festival of the anniversary of the spiritual Chief of our Mission Victor Hugo.

In the name of the caodaist hierarchy, I give you, Ladies and Gentlemen, our liveliest gratitude for your kind attention toward us.

You may, perhaps, have learned of the birth of Caodaism or Reformed Buddhism by publicity others than ours. You found that it was born of a marriage between Oriental and Occidental philosophy. It is the synthesis of all the faiths of the world.

What do we mean by Oriental philosophy ?

Is it not that which comes from high philosophical thinking of all the Asiatic religions most of them being found in China' except Buddhism which is of Indian origin, but which was also thousands years ago nationalized Chinese and Vietnamese.

The philosophy that forms the ground of Asiatic morals has already given to the Orientals several milleniums of civilization of which China is considered the guiding spirit. The Vietnamese nation profits greatly thereby.

Through the interpreter of Spiritism, we recognized that a reformation of the moral state of all humanity is necessary for the spiritual evolution of the world.

The human spirit had already come to a stage where the old dogmas and doctrines could not satisfy its freer and more sublime expansion. A new era must be reserved to it; that new era consists in giving it a broader horizon for its liberty of conscience. A new faith must be granted to it. That faith must comprise all other existing faiths, while conserving them in their philosophical purity. Hence the name of Caodài (High Church or Great Faith of the world) created by the Divine Spirit.

Caodaism or Reformed Buddhism practises a large tolerance toward all beliefs. It respects all human consciences as it respects the universal Conscience that is the emanation of God. The symbolic Eye figuring on our altar is the image of the individual Conscience and the universal Conscience. Our worship then is the worship of God and Humanity. The exterior manifestation of our new religion consists in bringing back all thoughts toward the primordial unity; « the Conscience in itself and the Conscience in God ». An inward voice makes us understand that Humanity is One; one in nation, one in thought, one in religion. The idea of uniting all mankind in a new conception of Love and Justice might give the world a more lasting peace by the practise of God.

Caodaism or Reformed Buddhism has a tendency to fraternize with all races and unify souls by preaching to the world Peace and Concord. Such are the great lines dictated by our divine Constitution practised by his ministers.

Holy see of Caodaism. — Principal Temple

Monumental Entrance, West side.

Principal Temple, front.

Interior of the Temple. Cao-Ðài's Altar. The Divine Eye, on the Universal Cosmos, at the location of the Polar Star, symbol of Religion, represents the Universal Conscience

Interior of the Temple. — Preceding the Divine Altar, situated on a platform, the seven seats of the greatest dignitaries, backs to the Altar.

1st rank : seats of the three Đầu-sư (Cardinals).
2nd rank : seats of the three Chưởng-Pháp (Censor-Cardinals).
3rd rank : Throne of the Pope.

I close, Ladies and Gentlemen, my dearest Brethren and Sisters in the faith, wishing that divine mercy may be spread on you and on the whole world ».

La Presse Indochinoise (5, 25th, 37), in a very long report, relates in detail the outstanding events of the ceremony. We extract only some new viewpoints ;

The dedication of the caodaist temple of PhnomPenh, celebrated three days ago, obtained a lively success among the population of the Khmer capital, and was marked with a character, at the same time splendid and solemn.

Thousands of spectators, the faithful, coming from Cochinchina and the remotest corners of Cambodia, invaded the temple till its compound become too narrow to contain the ceaselessly growing crowd.

For want of space, a dense throng stood along the sidewalks and on the curb of Đỗ-hữu-Vị Boulevard, which was filled with pedlars who did a thriving business. Yet, no unfortunate incident was noticed in the course of three days of festival ; the police force furnished by the caodaist members made it easy for the official police force. With a smile and every courtesy, they guided the guests and interested spectators.

In the evening, flags of different nations, pennants, banderoles, banners of various colours constituted a magnificent ornament, with the violently lit temple and agreeably decorated platforms where took place the reception of French and local authorities, representatives of the press and guests.

Inside the temple, the sanctuary, possessing an austere aspect, did not exclude beauty by its simplicity, On the right and left of the sanctuary were installed two altars : the one, of Quan-Thánh Đế-Quân ; the other, of Quan-Âm Bồ-Tát.

Outside, two big illuminated swastikas framed the symbolic Eye of which the pupil was lit by a green electric bulb. Opposite the temple, on the esplanade « Bạch-Vân » was erected a big altar with the photo of Victor Hugo seated, his elbow on a table, which was attended by two rows of members of three orders, in yellow, red, blue tunics.

In a broad court situated between the esplanade and the temple, numerous French, Cambodian, Vietnamese, Chinese and Hindu personalities visited various attractions, especially the fireworks, the dance of the unicorn, and the « long-mã » accompanied by Cambodian, French and Vietnamese music, which, vieing with each other in talent and ardour, produced and deafening uproar.

This speech was followed by a doctrinal discourse of great import delivered in Vietnamese by Mr. Phạm-công-Tắc who honoured the ceremony with his presence from the beginning. The end of the lecture was received religiously and with long applause by a fervent audience.

Truly, this inauguration of the temple marks a fine achievement for the Caodaists of PhnomPenh who did their very best to give their temple — formerly a simple straw hut — a worthy and admirable appearance.

La Dépêche (5, 26th, 1937) also gave a very detailed account, of which we shall cite only a few passages indicating new aspects of the ceremony.

On Pierre Pasquier boulevard, in the quarter that one of our collaborators not long ago called the « lake-dwellers city of Phnom-Penh », in the place of the little straw chapel dedicated to the new cult of Reformed Buddhism, the Caodaists of Cambodia have built a magnificent temple whose style strangely recalls that of Saint-Mexmes Church at Chinon ».

After a detailed description of the temple, we read :

« The Hộ-Pháp Phạm-công-Tắc who the day before had left the Vatican of Tây-ninh, and who stayed, on his arrival at Phnom-Penh, in the parish house erected within the circumference of the monastery, came at the appointed time to the temple, arrayed in the costume of a great marshall of the Celestial Empire, sheltered beneath golden parasols preceded by a band playing a lively march and escorted by a numerous retinue.

At the entrance of the temple, the Hộ-Pháp was welcome by the Chief of the Mission, surrounded by the local clergy. He was shown toward a platform of honour set back from the porch on which he stood during the ceremony, armed with his marshall's baton, the sight of which must have frightened the unhealthy spirits and kept them off the sacred place.

The smoke of the sticks of incense stuck into the vases of ash rose like a curtain before the symbolic globe and divinities.

The monks, draped in their red, blue or yellow gowns, the members dressed in their white robes, knelt on the mats in line and occupied the central and lateral naves of the temple. Now and then, heralds announced various phases of the ceremony at the top of their voices.

The festival over, the Hộ-Pháp was accompanied again by the same ceremonial to his rest house. He then had a quick interview with *La Dépêche* :

The Hộ-Pháp Phạm-công-Tắc is a keen, educated man ; he speaks and writes French admirably. He was reading *La Dépêche* when we were brought into the sitting-room by the Chief of the diocese. Immediately, he stood up, offered his hand like a gentleman and, with a smile, showed us to an arm-chair.

Fearing the torture of a long interview, he began to let us know that he was a faithfuf reader of our paper and took particular interest in its Cambodian edition for he had in the Khmer land more than forty thousand coreligionists.

For him Caodaism is a religion that draws its strength from social concord and peace. The benevolent hospitality that the Vietnamese Caodaists found in Cambodia touched him deeply. He wished with all his heart that his countrymen might witness their deep gratitude in regard to the local authorities by continuing to work, here as elsewhere, in the respect of the laws and customs of the country.

He manifested however his astonishment on seeing that orders, no doubt misinterpreted, had been given on the occasion of this festival, to keep the subjects of His Majesty Monivong from the merrymaking in the circumference of the Caodaist temple...

His Eminency Thượng-chữ-Thanh, Chief of the Foreign Mission, in residence at PhnomPenh, next took the floor.

First, he announced the death of Mrs. Lâm-ngọc-Thanh, a great dignitary of Reformed Buddhism, who had just died at Vũng-Liêm and asked the audience to observe a minute of silence.

Then he praised the founders of Caodaism in Cochinchina, particularly dwelling on the merits of the late Pope Lê-văn-Trung and another dignitary, the late lamented Cao-quỳnh-Cư. Afterwards, having concluded the account of the new religion in Cambodia, the orator informed the audience that the ceremony of inauguration of the temple of PhnomPenh coincided with the anniversary of the death of Victor Hugo, the spiritual Chief of the Foreign Mission of Caodaism.

Three other speeches delivered in Cantonese, Triều-Châu and Cambodian, reproduced almost word for word the speech of Mr. Thượng-chữ-Thanh.

In the afternoon, at 4.30 took place in the circumference of the monastery the procession of deified personages.

Preceded by a unicorn and followed by a dragon, the procession gathered in their order the car of Buddha Di-Lặc, an idol with a broad smile, impassible in his nirvanian happiness, the altar of the Pope Lê-văn-Trung, the portrait of Victor Hugo, the statue of Joan of Arc, the portrait of Cao-quỳnh-Cư, that of Sun-Yat-Sen, founder of the Chinese Republic, and at last the big car of the sacred Mountain on which sat enthroned the great sage Lý-thái-Bạch having on his right the goddess Quan-Âm and on his left the warrior Quan-Công.

At the foot of that mountain the late Pope Lê-van-Trung was blessing the crowd.

The procession, preceded, accompanied and followed by noisy orchestras, made three times the tour of the temple passing before the platform where were seated the Hộ-Pháp, the personages of his retinue and the dignitaries of the religion.

On a part of the platform, we noticed numerous Chinese women newly converted and draped in white cloaks like the Vietnamese, with the marks and badges of their grade.

In France, *Le Fraterniste*, in Cambodia, *La Vérité* (10,20th, 1937) published this impression of the whole :

The newspapers illustrations, the pictures that I have before me, show the unusual splendor of the festival that took place under the presidence of the Superior. Thousands of followers had come from all parts : fifteen, twenty, twenty-five thousand ? It is difficult to estimate such Asiatic crowds. Speeches were made and broadcast : by Charles, Chief of the Foreign Mission, by François, a guiding spirit of the movement. Those speeches reflect a number of ideas that seemed to me interesting.

The sponsorship of the spirit Victor Hugo should be sufficient to underline the eminently spiritualistic character of Caodaism, the actual Superior of which was the chief of the school of mediums at Tây-Ninh (Cochinchina).

The real alliance of the religions of the Orient and the religions of the Occident is affirmed there in every part, at every moment, for the Caodaist pagodas are open to the veneration of Christ, Buddha, Laotze, Confucius, Mahomet, and all the messengers of God on the earth, be they spiritualists (Victor Hugo, Camille Flammarion) or benefactors of humanity.

In an hour when some are putting a label on everything for dividing mankind and sowing hatred, it seems useful to encourage this movement of reconciliation, union, universality. In an hour when some go back to the exclusive formulas and anathemas of the years of old : « only here may you be saved », it seems good to repeat, even to the deaf, that it is forever finished with the pitiful game of labels : What only matters is not creeds, but acts. Allan Kardec has luminously expressed : outside of charity, no salvation.

The pacific and pacifistic spirit of Caodaism is also worthy approval. The disciples of Cao-Dài (the Supreme Being) are hostile to distinction of peoples, races, religions, colours, and wish a reconciliation of governments and the end of wars, which are always declared by governments. Facing the Occident, the Caodaits cry: we are for peace, fraternity of men, friendship of peoples, collaboration of races. Here we are far from the barbarous politics of totalitarian states, black, brown, or red pestilences, and hired adventurers who, in each country, seek to ape copying the new Badinguet.

One sees in it an admirable spiritualistic synthesis, where even an unbeliever finds his spiritual bread, because he may, in a Caodaist pagoda, ask the rules of conduct of Confucius or the sage Laotze. Indeed, the temple of Cao-Dài does not refuse its spiritual treasuries to anybody. May we be far from our label stickers, our little chapels, our small clans of benighted prefectures and sub-prefectures, dead dust.

The time-table enables us to understand the importance of these three days of festivals:

Program of May 21st, 1937

Morning :

5.15 a.m. Gathering of dignitaries and members at the temple.

5.30 a.m. Reception of H.H. Hộ-Pháp in the temple.

6. a.m. Great ritual ceremony and sanctification of the symbolic globe.

9. a.m. Reception of H.H. Hộ-Pháp on the esplanande of dignitaries and presentation of the sacerdotal body.

9.30 a.m. Songs and prayers by the children's chorus ; opening speech in Vietnamese by H.E. Thượng-chữ-Thanh, Giáo-Sư, Chief of the Foreign Mission; speeches in Chinese and Cambodian.

HISTORY AND PHILOSOPHY OF CAODAISM 95

Noon.
  11.30 a.m. *Prayer (at microphone) for world concord and peace.*
  Ritual ceremony and prayers for the dead.

Evening.
 4. p.m. Gathering of dignitaries on the esplanade.
 4.30 p.m. Procession of the portrait of Victor Hugo round the temple to be later installed on the esplanade « Bạch-Vân ».
 5.30 p.m. Ritual ceremony and prayers by the children's chorus ; lectures in Cambodian by Chánh - trị - sự Phạm-văn-Châu ; lectures in Vietnamese by Giáo-sư Hương-Phụng (Mme Trần-kim-Phụng), Tiếp-Đạo Cao - đức - Trọng and Khai - Pháp Trần - duy - Nghĩa. Speech in French by the Chief of the Foreign Mission.
 11. p.m. Great ceremony of the anniversary of Victor Hugo, spiritual Chief of the Foreign Mission of Caodaism.

Program of May 22nd

Morning.
 5. a.m. Ritual ceremony.
 8. a.m. Prayers for the repose of the dead and for world concord and peace.
 11. a m. Ritual ceremony.

Evening.
 4. p.m. Gathering of dignitaries on the Esplanade.
 4.15 p.m. Reception of H. H. Hộ-Pháp on the esplanade.
 5. p.m. Reception of French and local authorities, representatives of the press and guests.
 5.15 p.m. Prayer by children of the chorus in honour of the Religion : speech of inauguration of the Caodaist temple by the Assistant-Chief of the Foreign Mission (at microphone).

6. p.m. Vitsit of the temple by the Authorities and all the spectators.
6.15 p.m. Signing of the Golden Book.
6.30 p.m. Tea of honour.
8 p.m. Speech of H.H. Hộ-Pháp (H.H. Phạm-công-Tắc) (at microphone). Religious lectures by H. E. Thượng-Chữ-Thanh; other religious lectures.
11. p.m. Ritual ceremony.

Program of May 23rd.

Morning.
5 a.m. Ritual ceremony.
6 a.m. Gathering floats, votive tablets, dragons, unicorns, music, etc. on Pierre Pasquier Boulevard, opposite the Caodaist temple.
6.45 a.m. Start of the procession and train for town.
11. a.m. Ritual ceremony.

Evening.
4 p.m. Gathering of dignitaries on the esplanade.
4.30 p.m. Allotting of prizes for floats, dragons, unicorns, votive tablets, music.
5 p.m. Chants by the children's chorus in honour of the religion, with music; ritual ceremony.
6 p.m. Religious lectures by various dignitaries; closing speech by Tiếp-thế Lê-thế-Vĩnh.
10 p.m. Prayers in chorus for the repose of the dead and for world concord and peace.
11 p.m. Great ceremony of the 15th day of the 4th month of the year Dinh-Sửu.

Mr. Ch. Bellan, ex-Resident of France in Cambodia, sent from Paris (9, 1st, 37) his general impression:

« I read with great interest the documents you sent me, concerning the inauguration of the Caodaist temple of PhnomPenh.

I have shared them with some friends and personalities interested in this movement which tends toward the unification of religions and to universal fraternity.

In the course of history, the opposition of various religions has caused a great deal of bloodshed and one could wish that a mutual comprehension might be imposed for the happiness of humanity.

The progress of science has reduced distances more and more, but if the peoples of the earth understand each other a little better than formerly, it is no less true that they are often deceived by bad shepherds and that there exist, alas ! many misunderstandings among them.

If Caodaism spreads, we may expect an era of peace and quiet, if not of happiness, the latter being not of this world. Each one therefore must hoe his own row in that direction. For my part, I am truly very glad to know that the odious persecutions, of which the Caodaists have been the victims, is over.

One could not then, with the help of all, hinder the diffusion of a doctrine that might — as Buddha preached — it is not hate, but love that unites hearts — make calm to reign over the surface of this still-troubled earth.

My kind fraternal greetings.

Signed : Charles Bellan.

DOCTRINAL PRECISIONS

One of our good Caodaist brethren, Mr. Gabriel Abadie, of Lestrac, a little better informed than our great journalists of Paris (City of Light) presented in VU (September 7, 1932) a documentary and illustrated article on Caodaism contrasted with those who batten on error and lie, Mr. Abadie can prove how much he has suffered in committing himself to tell the truth about Caodaism.

« At the beginning of the year 1926, in a compartment situated in the vicinity of the « Halles Centrales », in Saigon, gathered some young learned men, all Buddhists, who were cultivating spiritism in their leisure hours. The idea had come to them from the sceances and revelations of one of their masters, a convinced spiritist and representative of the most important spiritist society of France.

The beginnings were not conclusive, but little by little, with the extreme patience which characterizes the Oriental, by eliminating those who did not possess « fluid », replacing them by comrades better endowed, they registered, it seems, extraordinary results.

They were, at the beginning, put in communication, they claim, with the spirit of one of the sages of Chinese Antiquity, Lý-thái-Bạch, more commonly called Li-tai-Pe, the Chinese Homer, he who reformed literature under the 13th dynasty Tang (713-742), an earnest Taoist who dictated them some messages. There were also those from Quan-Thánh-Đế-Quân, the Chinese Turenne. So, what seemed first to these neophytes of spiritism an amusement, rapidly became a mystic occupation: the conversation with superior spirits from Beyond from whom they took counsel.

But the use of the turning table to correspond with the occult world seeming to them impractical, this they confided to the Spirit, who recommended the billed-basket, a kind of rattan helmet, and at the same time counselled them to learn from the wisdom of one of their countrymen, the Phủ-Chiếu, a man versed in spiritism. The latter, who was following the doctrine of Gautama Buddha and practising the morals of Confucius told them that he had been in relations with the spirits for several years, from whom he had obtained this revelation : the existence of a Supreme Being, sovereign of the Universe, he was Cao-Dài. He taught the young men to use the *billed-basket* and participated in their spiritist sceances.

At the suggestion of the spirits, they entered into contact with one of their countrymen, a former Cochinchinese mandarin and member of the Government Counsel, Lê-văn-Trung, whose life of dissipation and unrestrained pleasure, did not predispose him to the part he was to be called to play.

Lê-văn-Trung's conversion was miraculous. Moved by grace, the opium-smoker smoked no more, the tippler abstained from his favorite alcohol, he ceased to eat meat and fish, gave up the pleasures of the flesh, became a vegetarian and practised the ascesticism of the austerest bonze. It was in a following and memorable meeting of spirits that the *billed-basket* enjoined Lê-văn-Trung to take up the propagation of Caodaism and conferred on him the title of Pope of the new religion.

On the subject of the universality of Caodaism, our brother very well explains the meaning of Cao-Dài :

« Cao-Dài is the symbolic name of the Supreme Being, who, for the third time, would reveal himself to the Orient.

The opinion of the followers of the new faith is that God, adapting his teachings to the progress of the human spirit, now more advanced than formerly, should this time be manifested through mediums, he being unwilling to allow any mortal the privilege of founding Caodaism. This new manifestation of the Supreme Being so comes because all religion submitted to human founder's authority is unsuited to universality, seeing that his prophets protested against the truths proclaimed by other religious faiths, toward which they show a marked intolerance.

The Caodaist doctrine is, in great part, drawn from the three principal and oldest religions of the Orient: Buddhism, Taoism, and Confucianism. It maintains their purest principles recognized as being the eternal, immutable truths of the Divine Law. But it intends to reestablish in their true meaning certain beliefs that seem to have been twisted.

So refounded, this doctrine conciliates all religious convictions and adapts itself to various degrees of spiritual evolution.

From a moral point of view, it reminds man of his duties and obligations, teaches him to know how to behave toward himself, his family, society, and the whole of Humanity.

From a philosophical point of view, it preaches contempt for honour, wealth, luxury, in a word, the freeing from servitudes of matter, to look to spirituality for the full quietude of the soul.

From the point of view of worship, it recommends the worship of God and the veneration of the superior spirits who constitute the occult August Hierarchy. It admits the cult of Ancestors, built upon the principles of Buddha, but stands out nevertheless against meat offerings and the use of votive paper.

From a spiritualist point of view, it agrees with other religions, on the existence of the soul, its survival from the physical envelope, its evolution by successive reincarnation, the posthumous consequences of human actions ruled by the law of Karma.

From the point of view of initiation, it preaches, to those of the followers judged worthy, the revealed teachings to empower them, by a process of spiritual evolution, to approach ecstasies of bliss.

The basis of caodaist doctrine is the practice of good and virtue. How could it be otherwise with a religion that amalgamates the three great systems of the Orient : Confucianism, Buddhism, and Taoism, in order to uphold only the highest teachings and eliminate the lower precepts considered as factors of superstition and ignorance ?

1º The *merciful Buddha* preached devotion and charity.

2º The *Taoist Doctrine* prescribed the worship of truth and the discipline of character.

3º The *sage Confucius* traced the way of the Golden Mean.

Cao-Dài united the great principles of love and goodness taught by the *Three Saints*, preaching a new religion wherein men of all colours must strive by new disciplines, toward the creation of a better world, of a world from which would be excluded wars and conquests and in which the races might fraternize ».

Our brother answers the objection of a certain journalist that Jesus Christ would be there only a second-rate divinity.

« Christ is a hyphen between Confucianism, Taoism and Buddhism. If he is placed below Far-Eastern divinities, it is because he came to the world many centuries later...

In 1932, Mr. G. Abadie had already foreseen the long and painful chapter of jokes and persecutions that were to be let loose and from which he would not himself escape.

« The new religion, Reformed Buddhism, did not raise, on account of the proverbial tolerance of the Far-Eastern peoples, any quarrel between the old worship and the reformed one, considering that it was not so intransigent as to declare that, besides its morals and doctrine, it could only have error and punishment. It shows on the contrary its respect for religions the teachings of which seemed to it worth veneration and it did not hesitate at all beside Buddha, Laotze and Confucius, to put in honour the image of Christ, wishing to spread a teaching, the origin of which troubled it less than its intrinsic value. There is nothing more to it except that the ground of its dogma is the law of the *Three-Saints* (Buddha, Lao-tze, Confucius) of which it conserves the old beliefs, habits and rituals.

One might ask oneself, especially these last years, what can be the deep causes that have put the native soul heretofore asleep, toward a religiosity reaching the mystic fanatism of the high periods of faith.

Why this religious awakening ? one asks.

The Caodaist doctrine tends to a moral and social action by making the Vietnamese people recover under the lead of their elite, the traditional taste of their simple, frugal and careful existence.

One wonders to see France or more exactly some over-zealous and certainly ill inspired officials take sides against the heretics of the reformed heathen religion in favor of, it seems, the old *belief, which, moreover, does not solicit it*, and require that the orthodox doctrine of the old Buddhism be respected without change, nor evolution of any sort that adapts it to new conceptions.

The explanation of the campaign conducted against Caodaism is found in the obstruction that gives rise to the reformed religion the number of faithful which is in Cochinchina, for instance, more than one million out of three million and a half inhabitants.

The former governor of Cochinchina Blanchard de la Brosse is now exposed to public opprobrium for having declared practicable, and authorized this religion in the territory under his jurisdiction. But the alarm is given and a crusade is launched against the heretics ».

Since then, great progress toward understanding has been accomplished, and Caodaism is on the way to becoming the official religion of the new State of Vietnam.

Le Cygne (Bạch-Nga, Hànội) published a series of articles : *The true visage of Caodaism* (9-36), from which we shall cite only the most curious passages. It was, as the title indicates an objective report. We can't pay a better compliment to it, for the truth is also God's service.

« Let my dear readers be assured! Instead of pulling a long face in reading the subject of this inquiry, looking me up and down with an astonished or sceptical or mocking eye, murmuring imprecations against me, let them listen calmly to the confessions of a man who, like them, and nearly all Tonkinese intellectuals, has willingly ridiculized a religion newly born in his own country, simply because he has understood nothing of it. « *Newly born* » is not quite the word; following the Caodaist calendar, Humanity is in the year of the 3rd Amnesty of God in the Orient; it is then ten years ago that this religion came into its own.

An experienced sociologist must notice that since the first quarter of this century, Vietnam has undergone an abrupt shock. There has been a complete overthrow of the destiny of people, its thought and faith. The return of the two Phan's (1) announced the first symptom of that fever which increases daily. From a political point of view, that is revolution in all minds and hearts. From an economic point of view, it is the intensive development of industry, the formation of cooperatives and syndicates. From a literary point of view, the radical reform of the language, the introduction of new concepts in Poetry and Art, and as for the domain of religion, the birth of a new faith. »

To the rebuke that Caodaism would be constituted only by ignorant and superstitious masses, skilfully shorn by swindlers and charlatans, this reply :

The thousands of Caodaist believers are not all credulous or superstitious persons. A great number of those who practise the new religion in Cochinchina, in Tonkin, in China, and in France, are intellectuals of the upper class, teachers, lawyers, writers, journalists, deputies. It is not without reason that Caodaism caused many to make mention of it throughout the world, that several famous reviews of Paris, London, Lisbon, Warsaw, even of Rome and of Buenos-Aires have started to study its dogma and doctrine. The author of this inquiry has had the rare privilege

---

(1) These are two great Vietnamese patriots: Phan-Châu-Trinh and Phan-Bội-Châu.

The tower dedicated to His Eminency Cao-Thượng-Phẩm, Supreme Chief of the Legislative Body of the monasteries (family name: Cao-quỳnh-Cư), great dignitary of the Body of Hiệp-Thiên-Đài, one of the founders of Caodaism (1887-1929).

Statute of Shakyamuni.

Legend tells how Shakyamuni fled from the Royal Palace of his father to devote himself to religion. The above photo shows Shakyamuni riding off on his horse; we also notice behind him, his chief valet imploring him to return to the Palace. Shakyamuni seeming hearing nothing, does not return.

Inside the Temple. On the occasion of the anniversary of the 61st birthday of H. H. Hộ-Pháp, Superior of Caodaism 61 candles are lit representing his age.

Prayers in common are said by all dignitaries and members of both sexes on behalf of the longevity of H. H. Hộ-Pháp.

Interior of the Temple. Seats of the three Principal Dignitaries of Hiệp-Thiên-Đài (Legislative Body) :
At the middle : Throne of H. H. Hộ-Pháp ;
On the right : Seat of H. E. Thượng-Sanh ;
On the left : Seat of H.E. Thượng-Pham (the latter disincarnated in 1929, has his statue in the place).

In the central nave of the Temple. — Dignitaries and members pray for the longevity of H. H. Hộ-Pháp on the occasion of the anniversary of His 61st birthday.

of ransacking the archives of the Holy See of TâyNinh where he could read letters and precious documents, bulletins of conversion addressed to the Pope by foreign personalities from different capitals of Europe and America. Even Japan, a country proud of its Bushido, has sent scholars to TâyNinh trying to understand what is this new faith which has shaken the world's opinion ».

La Vérité (The Truth), also, made a report (May 11, 13, 38) that was later put out in pamphlet form (special edition of this daily of PhnomPenh) and from which we note the following extracts:

« During the twelve years in which Caodaism has developed in Indochina, it is to be noticed that no serious objective study has yet been consecrated to it. However this social and religious movement touches hundreds of thousands of human beings on an ever widening scale. The new religion feeling itself cramped within the limits of its cradle, Cochinchina, has sent its missionaries to Cambodia, to Annam and to Tonkin, where it flatters itself with some success.

It has its temple in Paris, and ambition soon to bring the good word as far as China, Siam, India and Europe.

The Vietnamese pride is thus expressed unexpectedly in a field of action that was unknown to Giao-Chi's descendants. They brought nothing to human thought. Why? Mystery.

The Caodaism seems to despise the enigma so put, for it pretends to the dignity of religion at the same level as Buddhism. Moreover, is it not colled Reformed Buddhism ?

This ambition alone of the new faith that counts, it is said, millions of followers among which many intellectuals, induces us to study Caodaism carefully. Obeying to-day to the injunctions of friends, we have decided to present to the waiting public some truths about the new doctrine, some observations and objective analyses ».

La Vérité (The Truth)

In the preface of the pamphlet, the author adds these considerations :

« Some have loosed on the spiritist origins of the Caodaism much easy irony; they have tried to clothe off by ridicule, divine messages transmitted by the turning tables and the billed-basket.

What is there then surprising, unexpected, in the eternal truth borrowing that vehicle instead of making itself heard on a Sinai surrounded with lightnings and thunder, or expressing itself by the voice of inspired prophets or marvellous apparitions.

Do not the efforts of a medium, elected to that mission, as noble as any, isn't it at all so legitimate, offer as many guarantees as any voice chosen until the present to help Heaven to communicate with Earth ?

As for the persecutions of which Caodaism has been the object and of which the era is perhaps not closed, may we not see therein the better proof of its celestial origin and its supernatural character ? All religions preaching like it justice and goodness, founded like it on sacrifice and love, have known the hostility of man, the rancour of the powerful, the anger and reprobation of all those whose satisfied egos they came to trouble, whose authority they shook, whose pride and tyranny they combatted.

To be persecutor or persecuted, to dominate by force or to be a victim of violence, to impose faith by arms or to accept martyrdom, there is not, in all history, other alternative for growing religions. Had Caodaism any choice ? Its only weapon is gentleness. It could oppose to its enemies, but its resignation and confidence in the final triumph of justice; it could, on submitting itself to the laws, but proclaim, without weakening, its invincible attachment to the truth come from Above ; it could only endeavour to prove, by its firmness and constance, the authenticity of its divine mission. That is what it has done.

And its persecutors have been forced to bow before such heroic and quiet courage, to recognize its right to life, to grant it freedom, the only favor it claims.

Victorious over force, now disarmed, it remains to Caodaism to conquer the misunderstanding of men, their blindness, their scepticism. These are redoubtable enemies.

The other religions, of which it is the synthesis, have already confronted them. They have succeeded : Why should'nt it, too, succeed ?

Of what we can reproach it ? Too much good faith, too much sincerety, too much tolerance ? Is it for proposing an ideal too broadly, too fraternally human that we might reproach it ?

Is it at all contradictory in that fusion of diverse religions, each keeping, of its primitive faith, the essence and what forms for all a kind of common fund, that it must find means to make fraternity and the universal peace reign over mankind ? Here is how the Supreme Master, in one of his messages, explains the necessity of that fusion :

« Formerly, the peoples did not know one another and lacked means of transport : I then founded at different epochs, five branches of the Great Way : Confucianism, the Worship of geniuses, Christianism, Taoism, Buddhism, each based on the customs of the race called particularly to apply them.

« Nowadays, all parts of the world are exploited ; people knowing each other better, aspire to a real peace. But because of the very multiplicity of those religions, men do not live always in harmony one with another. That is why I decided to unite all those religions in one to bring them to the primordial unity.

« Moreover, the holy doctrine of those religions has been, through centuries, more and more denatured by those who have been charged to spread, up to such a point that I have now firmly resolved to come myself, to show you the way ».

It is then the whole world that now is offered to the apostolate of Caodaism, heir of the antique doctrines that have already conquered the quasi-unanimity of men.

The task shall be hard, for, as says the message we have just read, men have forgotten the very principles of the doctrines which they pretend to profess. They have sometimes conserved the letter ; but have more often lost the spirit.

The task shall be hard, for though the land where the missionaries must go to prepare the mission is no longer tillable, it is full of parasitic and poisonous plants as vigorous and solidly rooted as if all the evil human passions served them for manure. Never was the need more felt of reminding men that they all are sons of one Father and that the horrible fratricidal struggles, to which they gave themselves up yesterday, to which they are ready to submit to-morrow, shall cause the ruin and the sorrow not only of themselves, but of their children, and their children's children.

Caodaism is a synonym of peace, fraternity, love. May the millions of the believers it shall some day count, and may that be soon, remember to inspire their conduct by the eternal maxim, that is found in the books of the Masters of all times, in which are summed up all science and all wisdom: « Love one another ».

What is the point of view of the caodaist Sacerdocy on this report : it is *La Vérité* (The Truth) gives it to us.

« Our objective inquiry communicated to the orthodox Church of Caodaism has earned from its greatest Chief, the Superior Phạm-công-Tắc, the charming letter from which we cite below an excerpt concerning the relation of the Đại-Đạo to *Minhlism*.

Our readers shall understand by this simple letter the broad tolerance of the Caodaist spirit, which rejects no belief on account of its non-conformity or its non-orthodoxy. Such an attitude honours the Caodaists, notwithstanding all other social and philosophical considerations.

Ed. Note

Phạm-Công-Tắc, Superior of Caodaism or Reformed Buddhism, Holy See at TâyNinh, to the Director of *La Vérité*, PhnomPenh.

Mr. Director,

« The caodaist Sacerdocy and I are deeply touched by your high token of sympathy toward our religion : We have read your report with interest. Further, it is the only organ that has courageously defended our cause since the beginning. We can say that it is our friend. This report is interesting from any point of view, save some little errors of documentation of which we beg you to be so kind as to grant us hearing.

« Caodaism does not spring from the Minhlist movement. We recognize that the Minh-Lý was organized before us, but it is separated from us by a mystic and philosophical point of view. The truth is that the Vietnamese spiritualist movement came into being spontaneously with the help of no foreign concept, doctrine or dogma. It was unforeseeable. We can say that it was almost miraculous. As if led by an invisible power, the manifestation is latent. Moreover, this movement has been felt in all the world. All the spiritualist organizations that were created after the war were perhaps born of that unknown power.

« As for the Caodaists, a group, of intellectuals gathered to search for the possibility of harmonizing the two civilizations, the Oriental and the Occidental.

« They have tried in this case to bring close the two philosophies : Christianity and Confucianism. The attempt is so encouraging by reason of the high morality of the great thinkers who thus converge toward the Good and the Beautiful. There exists, then, a spot where ideas can meet and thus thoughts be united. Knowing this, the group of Vietnamese Intellectuals took steps to prepare a field of mutual understanding. They have begun very modestly first by making a comparison between two philosophies while looking for an intermediary. They have had the satisfaction to see great ideas can no longer separate thinkers of the human race. Morals are one, it is only practise that differs. Here is to them an obstacle or a catch. The power to act is not within the reach of common men such as they. It is above their reach. A bit of slowing down was seen in the Caodaist movement. These intellectuals seek for a way : unity of faith and practise of all religions.

« Without my describing it, you can guess the value of such an attempt.

One of their friends came from France in the person of Captain Monnet. He is a spiritist. He took interest in the researches of these intellectuals, but friendly understanding in the practise of all religious faiths escaped from him too. He advised them to consult the Spirits. That is to say they have had recourse to the help of the Beyond to solve their difficulties. The first spiritist communication, given by the Spirits, in the form of a counsel, gives them the key to the enigma.

« The conclusion is this: Faith derives from the Conscience, the Conscience is impossible of subordination. It differs according to the state of the spirit of each individual. It is impersonal and inalienable, because it is God's emanation (the universal Conscience). So, a liberty of conscience for all human beings is proclaimed, but union in the spirit of the Beautiful and the Good is obligatory, from which was born the Caodaist doctrine: the doctrine of broad tolerance.

One might say that Caodaism is a purely philosophical religion, whereas the Minh-Lý is a body that limits itself to a cultural practice of the three Oriental religions: Buddhism, Taoism and Confucianism, mixed a little with hypnotical mysticism.

It is a friend to Caodaism in its social manifestation, but it is not a blood brother.

We hope to be able to meet it in the practise of the Beautiful and the Good of which we make an apostolate of propaganda ».

Signed : Phạm-công-Tắc.

And here is one of the famous spiritualistic seances at the beginning of Caodaism :

It was in 1926, I was living in an apartment of the Audouit building, now become the Huỳnh-đình-Khiêm building. At my home, there came in and out young boys and girls, students, republicans, progressionists and revolutionary militants.

One Sunday morning, an unknown young man came into my office, took a seat opposite me and blurted out, without ceremony, these words which, however, did not astonish me: I have been, in fact, accustomed to this kind of visit and proposition.

— My dear friend, if you like, we are going to strike up a friendship to study philosophy and politics together. You know, no doubt, better than I, what relation these two activities have to each other.

In the feverish social and political atmosphere in which we lived at that time, which seems already strangely distant, I did not wonder either to read on my caller's card ; Vietnamese Revolutionist.

On the evening of the day before appearing for the examination for the first part of his B.A., this good boy was expelled from school. His crime ? To have written to Mr. Cognacq, at that time Governor of Cochinchina, to protest against a certain speech of his. Since that moment, this student had set himself to read enormously; to steep himself in various philosophical systems ; to be convinced of the necessity of a revolution. To manifest his new faith, he did not hesitate to have his calling-cards printed as I have showed above...

The fanatics of my friend type were so numerous that I didn't suspect him to be a provocateur. Later I found that my new friend was highly educated ; that he was versed in spiritualistic philosophies and that « spiritism » interested him particularly. That is how I was led to know the movement of turning tables and medium communications. One evening in November, my friend was reminding me for the Nth time of the marvels of turning tables, which he had learned from the works of some promoters of French Spiritism, now departed, Allan Kardec and Léon Denis. I threw out a categorical challenge as to the veracity of these phenomena, defying to attempt an experiment: He brought me at once to some authentic chiefs of an occult school at that time newly born, the later activities of which were to have a great influence on the formation and development of Caodaism : his school was called Minh-Lý-Đạo, which may be literally translated : *The Way of Enlightened Reason.*

I hasten to acknowledge that I was placed in the presence of extremely kind and honest men. They were humble employees in administration and business, eager for self-improvement and rising in society thanks to their continued efforts. They were ten who gathered in a kind of coterie to discuss spiritualistic philosophies, and then when the theories were well asssimilated to a new canon they created themselves, with a view to venerating their saints and sages.

I was very surprised at their broad spiritualistic learning. They all were capable of citing for me entire passages of the greatest works of the spiritists. Better than their French Masters, they had the audacity to use Henri Durville, the renowned occultist, in their pursuit of truth.

That is how one of the leaders, Mr. Xứng, kindly inaugurated the author's relationship with his group by a hypnotic experience. I confess, however, that I found in it nothing truly conclusive.

After having me shut my eyes, he made various movements in the air with their two broad hands all around my head without ever touching it. After a quarter of an hour of this hypnotic preparation, he ordered me with a clear and caressing voice to incline my head in a certain direction, or to make certain gestures with my arms, which I did without difficulty.

The spectators who were members of the group and my friend X were visibly satisfied with the experience : As I insisted on attending a seance of some importance, Mr. Âu-Kích, the most esteemed of the group, prepared it.

On a table used as an altar, he had nine candles placed triangularly : He then explained to me that the figure nine as well as the geometrical placement imply the number three (three angles in a triangle, actually) and have a symbolic importance, that only the initiate can understand. Then began the ceremony of offerings.

The members of the group prostrated themselves before the altar, the chief, Mr. Âu-Kich placing himself in the middle. They recited prayers to the Author of Creation and the gods. After the offering of their hearts, it was flowers, tea and alcohol. I noticed in their prayers the recognized themes of various Asiatic religions. Besides, their catechism does not hide the fact that their philosophy is a synthesis of the Buddhist, Confucianist and Taoist religions. But here it was suddenly, that the chief drew strange movements in space with his right arm. All fell silent as if by magic. — X. whispered in my ear that the « Spirits » were going to make a communication through Mr. Âu-K'ch.

In fact, the latter having seized a big pencil which had been placed beforehand on a small table with some paper, set to transcribe the divine words, his eyes closed. They explained to me that he was the preferred « medium » of great spirits; venerated by the faithful, which the Bodiseatva Quan-Âm had dedicated to me through the chief of the group. I was, in fact, very proud to learn that during my « former existences » I had accomplished great works, and I was « exiled in this valley of tears » only to atone for the crime of pride of which I was guilty. I should have been an unbearably proud man « in the course of my successive existences ».

This my friends believe in mediumnity, that is to say in communications with the « Beyond » and consequently in the survival of the soul. Differing from the Catholics, they do not speak of eternal hell, but about transmigration of the soul, which, by leaving, the physical body, may live in other earths than ours. In this, they resemble the Buddhists, with, however, this important restriction : whereas Shakyamuni's disciples admit that a human soul may come back to the earth and live in the body of a beast, Minh-Lý's followers, more modern, reject this hypothesis. In their new faith, the law of attraction replaces, in very unexpected fashion, the Buddhist transmigration of the soul. It is unnecessary then to have the wicked come back to this earthly life in the skin of a pig or a dog to atone for past faults: This would be moreover presenting the Author of Creation as too cruel a judge. No, the law of attraction, that plays in space, suffices for celestial justice. Such, who through a life of sacrifices should be « deified » after death, thanks to the attraction, arrive at a superior world in space. On the contrary, the wicked, the selfish « shall fall themselves », after their departure from the earth, into a planet whose conditions of existence are still more painful. All this is done naturally, automatically, « as it were » :

Though these latter lines are not very clear, or are disputable from a latin spiritualistic point of view (the Anglo-saxon spiritism does not admit of a return to the earth, but of progress in spheres of space), let us come to the « utility » of Caodaism :

« Nevertheless with the triumph of capitalism, the old Cochinchinese patriarcal economic structure was broken down. The Gia-long Code which recognized only the collective personality of the village and the family, thoroughly anti-individualistic, was abolished or almost so, in Cochinchina, where the individual freedom recognized more or less by the modified codes is the cause of the discard of Confucianism. After all, the latter has really constituted a religion with its Canon, its clergy, its temples, and not just a morality.

It is clear that under these conditions, a father's authority as well as that of a husband or a landowner, could be more threatened in Cochinchina than in other parts of Vietnam where the Gia-long Code and Confucianism still retain their power. That is, in my opinion, the only reason why there was room in our twenty Cochinchinese provinces for the birth of a new faith.

If the Shakyamuni doctrine can be subdivided into two great schools : that of the Greater Vehicle also called « Northern » which comprises in Indochina the Vietnamese Buddhist population, and that of the Lesser Vehicle or « Southern », which influences Cambodia and Laos, why should it not be able to take upon itself the modern form of Caodaism ?

We pass by all that is connected with the persecutions in this pamphlet.

Concerning the future of Caodaism, two remarks:

1) Whatever one may say about Confucianism, it was the «national religion» of China and Vietnam. In these countries, the spiritual and the temporal powers are joined in one man's hand, the Emperor's, the Son of Heaven, consequently, master of soul and body of his subjects. To have religion, there must be temples of worship or churches; a canon; a clergy. These conditions have been met by the Nho doctrine. The temple of worship, is it the paternal house itself? While the «four classics» and the «five canons» sum up the catechism of the «Saint of the land of Lỗ», Confucius. The clergy was a society of men of letters who, in fact, held both powers, spiritual and temporal, with, as a kind of Pope, the Emperor, the Son of Heaven.

The development of capitalism in Cochinchina with its consequent abrogation of the Gia-long Code, an abrogation that favours individualism to the detriment of Confucian collectivism, undermined favourable conditions to the survival of the religion of the sages. It is thus, historically, that the dawn of new religious sects, and particularly of Caodaism, must be explained.

2) It is characteristic in our century of international capitalism, this religious Reform of ours is contemporary with an Asiatic movement of the same essence, the same historic mission. For, in Japan and China, the tormented elements of the feudal bourgeoisie seek to create a social superstructure by founding a thousand and one modern neo-buddhist sects. The Caodaists and Minhlyists of our country will profit by comparing their doctrines with those of the Japanese and the Chinese Reforms.

I add that the Minhlý was but a new sect among many other sects that grew like mushrooms. But it represented the sect the most disciplined, the most educated from a philosophical point of view, and which possessed a theory wholly expressed in its catechism.

Caodaism (literally: religion of the High Throne), the founder of which was the late Lê-văn-Trung, quickly made contact with Minhlyism to borrow its theory, its worship, its ritual organization. But while Mr. Âu-Kích's proud school tends only to form an elite, Caodaism addresses itself to the masses. Thus, it represents the characteristic features of a religious organization of the mass.

The diversity and multiplicity of new religious schools which have appeared in Cochinchina since 1926 are characteristic of our epoch of free and intensive thinking. We do not count the sects any more ; let us mention only the most important ones : Minh-Lý, Minh-Thiện, Minh-Tân, Cao-Đài. The latter is subdivided into orthodox and un-orthodox schools. Besides the churches of the « Reformed Buddhism » which have some right to pretend to the dignity of a philosophy, we notice the birth of sects with strange practises. These are, no doubt, Chinese romantic reminders. Thus, we have seen General Nguyễn-văn-Điền with his disciples in open battle with the orthodox religion of TâyNinh. Questioned by the authorities regarding the attempted violation of the Caodaist « Holy Land », all refused to talk.

Also curious is the Nguyễn-kim-Muôn school, which does not fear to express in scarcely veiled terms, beliefs related to Mahometan sensualism.

All the sects of which we speak above were born almost simultaneously. All, without exception, claim to be a reform of Buddhism judged to be out of date.

Surprisingly, Cochinchina, alone of all the countries in the union, took the initiative in this kind of religious Reform which furthermore, participates in, perhaps without knowing it, the widest and most general movement that includes China and Japan.

In fact, in those countries, and particularly in the land of the Rising Sun, we notice the beginning of a thousand and one neo-buddhist sects that practise spiritism. Professor Chamberlain has exposed to the European public the various philosophies of the Japanese religious movement.

Caodaism by its originally spiritualistic character is confused with certain new religious tendencies of China and Japan of an occultist character.

We have before our eyes documents which admit of no doubt : « China, for many centuries, has known spiritualistic seances » (*Psychic News*, London, 4-8-39). « Worship of spirits and practises of sorcery » (*Opinion*, Saigon, 7-1-37). « The Dalai-Lama spoke in a German dialect » (*La Ricera Psichica*, Milan, 11-38). « Toward the religious renaissance in Japan » (*Vers une économie fraternelle*, Kagawa p. 18). « Astral projection, automatic writing, dematerialization : The Baron of Meck proves that it is in China people experiment the best mediums » (*The Two Worlds*, Manchester, 12-16-38). Pearl Buck declares that the Orient and the Occident must combine » (*The New York Times Magazine*, 11-20-38). « The Massacre of Animals » (by Jews) (*The Two Worlds*, 7-7-39). « A German scientific expedition in China and Siam » (*Gazette de Hongrie*, Budapest, 10-29-38). « The festival of Wesak (Great Buddhist Feast)» (*The Occult Review*, London 1939, p. 167). « The survival of the past among the Japanese » (*Tribune de Genève* 4-25-39). « The « Kuatsu » or the Japanese art of restoring the dead to life » (*O Astro*, St Paul, Brazil, 10-38). « Spiritism in China They resuscitate the dead »! (*The Two Worlds*, 7-14-39). The Shinto (*Revue théosophique*, Paris 12-35) « Confucius, Laotze and the afterlife » (*Light*, London, 7-20-39). Buddhism in North India, and Burma (*Light*, 7-20-39) ; etc. etc.

But opposition between the European spirit and the Asiatic religious conceptions often break out.

In the *Nouvelle Revue* (9-1-35), we can read the confusion of it in the book: *Buddhism*, by Entai Tomomatsu.

In presenting the book, *Buddhism*, of his friend Entai Tomomatsu, the translator, Mr. Kui Matsuo, himself the author of the *Japanese Buddhist Sects*, as well as numerous works of philosophy and of delicate translations, Mr. Matsuo writes ; « This book is not the scholarly work of a specialist, but merely a work intended for modern men and sceptical intellectuals. »

In spite of the simplicity with which the doctrine of Buddhism is exposed, it does not seem to us that this work and especially the philosophy which he attempts to bring within the scope of the average intelligence, can deeply penetrate the European masses, the principle of the « non-self » and that of causality, as conceived by the Buddhists being found, for the Occidental mentality, too much in opposition to the conception of the majority, that will always prefer to cast upon that entity, under the name of « Destiny », the responsibility of their sufferings, rather than acknowledge « the natural harvest of grain sown ». That wich, in Mr. Entai Tomomatsu's work, seemed able to retain our attention most particularly is, besides Buddha's psychology, to which the author restores his profoundly human sense, the statement of the attempt made by certain Japanese intellectuals to bring Buddhism back to its original nobility by freeing it from the conceptions of certain interested sects, which, for believers, prayer, meditation with crossed legs and especially offerings, contitute the essential.

That movement, to which we cannot help giving all our sympathy and which relies on the fact that Buddha, since his satori (illumination) always attached more punyas (merits) to the social act than to the most earnest prayer, the most severe mortification, that movement, even if it must remain purely Asiatic, is yet worthy to be known by us, for, permitting the adaptation of Buddhism to the practical life, it could be very heavy with consequences in the whole world.

And if we consider that no text exists, facilitating the knowledge of Buddhism, we must thank Mr. Entai Tomomatsu and his faithful translator for having given us that work by way of introduction to the study of a philosophy able, so says the author, to penetrate not only into an epoch, but all epochs.

The opposition breaks out, still more brutally, in such an echo as this : The secrets of the '(Mahatmas » in Brazil.

« While the *Bulletin des Amitiés Spirituelles* (No 40, page 17) sets itself to depreciate the « faith » of the « superhumans » and to reduce them to proud little Luciferians compartmented in a corner of the Created and wishing to dethrone God (sic). *O Pensamento,* Saint Paul's great initiatic review passes in review the faculties developed by those «initiates» despised by Sédir (p. 396) and his christic sect.

1) Possibility of entering into relations with the planetary beings of the solar system;

2) Our cosmos has no more secrets for them because of their internal vision;

3) Knowledge of the future;

4) Possibilities of acting on matter;

5) Transmission of sound to great distance;

6) Limited influence upon the actions of other men;

7) Reading of others' thoughts;

8) Spontaneous understanding of all languages;

9) Possibility of prolongation of the physical life (Elixir of a long life);

10) Healing of sick persons;

11) Power of duplication, etc.

For despicable little «Initiates», confined in a small corner of the Created, that is not so bad!

But what is painful — and with which people play — is to oppose these possible faculties of the «Mahatmas» to Christ's virtues, to denounce them as incompatible, in order to succeed by «cultivated ignorance» to maintain the party spirit, instead of opening their arms to all men, without category or distinction! Though some be not ready for that universal embrace, we see that by limitation, being prejudiced, they try to impose it upon others.

O Astro (5-1-39) has estimated that in 1926, there still were in Japan 71,281 Buddhist temples frequented by 58,621,000 inhabitants. Where is Christianity in the Nippon Archipelago? According to *La Luz del Porvenir* which borrows the details from the great spiritualistic association *Oomoto Internacia* (in Esperanto) we believe now dissolved, and its leaders hunted down and incarcerated. Sixty years of evangelization by missionaries have succeeded in converting only 250,000 Japanese, a stable figure in spite of thee normous increase in population these last years. At the same time, new sects and religions with a Buddhist and Shintoist basis draw to themselves thousands and thousands of new believers : Comoto, for instance, counts more believers than Christianity.

A man to all men must say :

Li-Tai-Pe was for China what Homer was for Greece and Ossian for Scotland.

Quan-thánh-Đế-Quân was for China what Turenne was for France.

Buddha, Laotze, Confucius were what They are and Thee, Thou art a son of God as I am thy brother. Thy suffering is my suffering. Let my joy in being a son of God be thy joy in being my brother.

Buddha, Laotze, Confucius were what they are and thou, and I, are sons of God. So as for Thee, thou art I and I am thee. If thou understandest that, afterwards thou shalt understand peace, harmony and the joy of being.

Anniversary of the 61st birthday of H. H. Hộ-Pháp. H. H. Hộ-Pháp coming down from the esplanade to preach before the microphone. The dragon-horse bearing the attributes of the Universal Peace, dances and precedes the procession.

The 61st birthday of H. H. Hộ-Pháp. H. H. Hộ-Pháp preaches and sends his greetings to the spectators.

Anniversary of the 61st birthday of H. H. Hộ-Pháp. Caodaist dignitaries respectfully listen to the sermon given by H. H. Hộ-Pháp

Anniversary of the 61st birthday of H. H. Hộ-Pháp. The crowd acclaims H. H. Hộ-Pháp who is already on the esplanade.

Central nave seen from the altar. — Notice the two praetoriums built against two columns surrounded with dragons. The right praetorium is reserved for gentlemen-dignitaries and the left one for lady-dignitaries.

Caodaist Holy see. — Visit and reception in the Temple of E.H. Trần-văn-Hữu, President of the Government of Vietnam, of Mr. Pignon, High Commissioner of France for Indochina and various civilian and military personalities from Saigon.

CAODAIST RITUAL

The Holy See of TâyNinh gathered in a pamphlet various pages of the Revue Caodaiste *(Caodaist Review)* and published in 1936 under the title « Caodaism or Reformed Buddhism » (3rd amnesty of God in the Orient), with these words of introduction :

« The pages you are going to read are extracted from the *Revue Caodaiste,* published at Saigon.

We have been very careful to gather, classify and coordinate them into a small pamphlet that shall present to the reader a summary statement of the scheme and the doctrine of Caodaism or Reformed Buddhism.

May these modest selections help the seeker after Truth to have an exact idea about the Caodaist ideal in its principal traits ».

The Caodaist Sacerdocy.

We can perhaps notice already that prayer constitutes the most important part in the Caodaist worship: Here is how the Caodaist Dignitaries justify it:

« We are reproached for being uselessly absorbed in long prayers, taking much time for this obligation which might be better employed otherwise, We should willingly acknowledge the cogency of the grounds for this reproach if the prayers we practise consisted in a monotonous recital of intelligible words from which the thoughts of the heart were excluded. But practised with intelligence and earnestness, energetic and full of unction, a prayer, an act of faith, is not only an act of worship, but also an elevation of the heart, a spring of the soul toward the Supreme Being.

In the existing state of their religious evolution, the mass of the Caodaist faithful need to acquire a will such as will permit them to resist material temptations under all circumstances, and to surround themselves with pure atmosphere which wards off bad ideas and inferior influences of space.

That will, to be efficacious, must be sustained by faith. Now the repeated practise of prayer strengthens that so precious faith, at the same time attracting, by the purity of the heart, the protecting forces of the Beyond. Further, there is nothing more ravishing, more sublime than examining one's conscience, forgetting everyday, by hours of fervent prayer, business and the world, to lift one's thoughts toward God with Which one deals face to face.

Such is the aim of a prayer that must be daily practised by the simple faithful. To-morrow, raised to a superior degree of evolution, they shall know how to bring it back to its abstract, interior form: meditation.

From an invocatory point of view, we pray for sick, unhappy persons, for which we beg God, not the enjoyment of a material good, of a personal interest, but the prompt return to health or the favour of an occult moral support, empowering them to undergo, without weakness, a trial or a karmic consequence.

We also pray for the suffering, unhappy spirits, for whom we invoke divine mercy.

Thus performed, prayer constitutes one of the necessary practises for the salvation of souls.

They who have some religious experience, who speak about religious things not from *the outside* (as one curiosity that is well worth another: the point of view of Parisian journalists, in general), but from *the inside*, shall recognize a great wisdom in these simple lines.

The Caodaist Symbolism

From the same pamphiet, we quote these passages (p. 21): « From the consciousness that man has duties toward Got that created him, is born the feeling of adoration. The whole of the acts by which we witness to God that feeling of adoration constitutes what we call worship. This is true of Caodaist worship. This is practised everyday, in temples as in private homes, in four sessions (tứ-thời): at six o'clock a.m., at noon, at six o'clock p.m., then at midnight. Prostrated before the divine altar, in the leap of the soul toward the Supreme Being, we begin with the rite of the offering of incense (niệm-hương). Then comes that of the opening of prayers (khai kinh).

Those prayers once said, we set ourselves to sing in chorus a song to the glory of God, then three others in honour of The *Three Saints*.

Such is, in all its simplicity, the rite of daily worship. As for the divine worship celebrated in temples on the days of great ceremony, there is a more imposing ceremonial.

The dignitaries of the male sex, in their costume of ceremony, the colour of which is determined by the branch to which they belong, prostrate themselves in transversal rows, on the mat spread before the divine altar which they face. On their right and before the altar of Quan-Thánh-Đế-Quân, kneel on another mat the followers of the same sex (Nam-phái) all dressed in white with the traditional black turban on their heads.

On the left and facing the altar of Quan-Âm-Bồ-Tát, prostrated in the same manner as their fellow-worshippers on the right, are the women (Nữ-phái) also dressed in white : as for dignitaries, they are distinguished from the simple believers by their special costume.

Prayers are everywhere the same ; but here, they are set to music and recited according to command given by the masters of ceremony (Lễ-Sanh).

The Caodaist worship, besides constituting an act of adoration, contains a symbolism, which in brief, we will explain to our readers :

The disposition of the altar, such as described by Mr. G. Coulet, is but the symbol of the fusion in unity of five branches of the Great Way (Ngũ-Chi Đại-Đạo). But the objects of worship, the offerings, etc... bear a secret seal, a symbolic meaning.

The objects of worship. — In the middle of the altar, is constantly kept lit a lamp with a spherical glass (Thái-Cực Đăng) symbolyzing the Universal Monad (Thái-Cực).

In the beginning of the ages, the Universe, we think, was constituted by the Monad, who is the Universal Soul, the non-manifested form of God.

By his manifestations, the Monad successively presented his two aspects male and female (Lưỡng-Nghi) represented on the altar by two kindled fires (Lưỡng-Nghi Quang).

Offerings. — The offerings of flowers, alcoho land tea, respectively symbolize the three constitutive elements of the human being : the Tính, the Khí and the Thần.

The Tính, as its name shows, is the essence of all matter, the cosmic sperm, without which no light may be manifested. It is the sexual energy of man and animal, the germinative virtue of plant. By its evaporation, the Tính, which resides in man, constitutes the coarse part of the perispirit. It is to the perispirital body as the flesh is to the physical body.

The Khí, which literally means breath, air, is in man, health, strength, vital energy. It is in the perispirit, the agent that unites the soul with the physical body, which it vivifies.

The Thần, intelligent principle, is double in the human being, the superior mental (dương-thần or hồn) is the divine Spirit in man ; the inferior mental (âm-thần or phách) is the most subtile part of the perispirit.

To convert sexual energy into vital energy (luyện tinh hoá khí), vital energy into mental energy (luyện khí hoá thần), such is the processus of the mystical purification of the three constitutive elements of the human being.

As for the sticks of incense we burn at each ceremony, they are invariably five. Now this symbolic number represents the five degrees of Initiation :
1) Giải-Hương : purity (Shila) ;
2) Định-Hương : meditation (Dhyana) ;
3) Huệ-Hương : wisdom (Prajna) ;
4) Tri-kiến-Hương : superior knowledge (Djnana) ;
5) Giải-thoát-Hương : karmic liberation (Apavarga).

To be admitted to the threshold of Initiation, the first condition for the worshipper is purity in all its form : purity of body, action, language, and thought.

Once the threshold is crossed, he sets himself to meditation. By this spiritual exercise, the believer whose thoughts and sensations stand aloof from the world of sense, lifts his soul toward the Superior Self, with which he is put into close contact. In the tête-à-tête of this inner withdrawal carried the completest possible abstraction where the human soul seeks to identify itself with the universal Soul, truths shine little by little into the worshipper's spirit, no longer, lured by the illusory appearances of anything in the world.

At the highest degree of ascension, he feels in his being the full wakening of the superior knowledge that permits him to perceive all eternal truths and embrace, without the least effort, the whole of the past and future. In this state of supreme wisdom, he can contemplate without being dazzled, the divine Light, a light that purifies, illumines and beautifies. Before him, the way of salvation is now open: the karmic liberation.

From that symbolism, as simple as powerful, emanates the great constructive and universal lesson of the human brotherhood ;

« It is important for the good of bruised and suffering humanity, that every people forget its personal interest to think but of those of the whole ; that they forgive one another in all manifestations of thought and faith ; that they at last show to one another the broadest tolerance. You may object that in the actual state of human mentality, more prone to egoism than altruism, talking about universal fraternity, is equivalent to dreaming of utopia. This objection is unfortunately plausible and shall remain such, so long as man shall be conceived as a *body* rather than a spirit ; « for, said Annie Besant, matter grows by taking round it, constantly adopting what is exterior to it, and incorporating it into what it already possesses. Material things are worn out and finally perish in the use, and as their quantity is limited, they who desire to possess it are numerous, struggles spring up between these latter. Earning, possession are in effect the conditions of material success.

« But when man begins to conceive himself as a spirit rather than a body, he understands that dividing and giving are the conditions of growth and power. Spiritual riches increase in fact in the use ; they never perish ; when they are given, they are multiplied ; when they are divided, their possession, their assimilation but become more complete. Brotherhood must come from the Spirit and be spread outside, through domains of intellect and emotion, to finally affirm themselves in the material world. It shall never be established by law imposed from outside, it must triumph by the Spirit overflowing from within ».

One day, the petty king Cung-Vương of Sở's principality lost a hunting crossbow. His officers were ready to go and seek it, but Cung-Vương prevented them, saying : « What is the use of fetching it. Bear in mind that we don't lose anything ; when a crossbow mislaid by an inhabitant of Sở is soon found again by another inhabitant of the same principality ». Confucius having heard those words, commented : « What a regrettable limitation in Cung-Vương's feeling of fraternity ! Would he not better have said : *a man lost a crossbow, another man shall find it.* ». So expressed, the concept of human fraternity by the great Chinese philosopher appears more beautiful, more striking, more concise ».

On this splendid plane of human fraternity, Christ disciples and Hiram's sons, the followers of Buddha, Confucius, Laotze and enthusiasts of theosophy, spiritism, and occultism, find themselves united in their common desire to build the Temple of Humanity. Let us help with all our might, this fraternal union, this constructive cooperation, that we no longer need blush for the crimes and atrocities with which we have till now bloodied so many centuries of History! It is time, past time, to redeem so much of barbarity.

Let us pray! meditate! become living temples.

To reach summits, after trials, a Caodaist disposes of the « Cell of meditation » :

The cell of meditation is a place where faithful are admitted to receive Initiation.

Every believer who asks to be admitted there, must conform to the following rules :

Art. 1. — He must have fulfilled his moral duties (Nhon-đạo) and an exclusively vegetarian diet for more than six months.

Art. 2. — He must be presented by a member more virtuous than he.

Art. 3. — All written communication with the outside shall be forbidden to him, except with his parents, on condition that it be read beforehand by the Superior of the institution.

Art. 4. — He must refuse access to the establishment to all strangers to the religion, though they be officials or members of his own family.

Art. 5. — He is forbidden to converse with persons from outside ; however, he may receive the call of his parents or children with the Superior's authorization.

Art. 6. — He must abstain himself from chewing betel, smoking tobacco and eating anything besides meals served by the institution.

Art. 7. — He must have a calm spirit, a quiet conscience. He must live on good terms with his cell-mates and avoid loud conversation ; he must help them in religious practise.

Art. 8. — He must obey all injunctions of the Superior and practise spiritual exercises following the scheduled prescriptions fixed by the latter.

How many Occidentals give themselves up to prayer ? I mean a free and spontaneous prayer.

How many Occidentals give themselves up to meditation ?

Yes, I repeat : in spiritual matter, we Occidentals are illiterates.

Even if the great Architect of the Universe was but an illusion, a lure, a word, prayer should be useful, meditation should be useful. In our crass, in our antireligious frenzy, we have banished both from our daily practises, from our spiritual exercises of everyday! But here, perhaps, a new science ; Cosmobiology (with its great poet : Théo Varlet), brings us back softly, not to frighten us. Strong spirits are gentle people, who do not like to be cheated.

Counsels to a Caodaist of Europe

Reformed Buddhism is broad tolerance, it is the junction of all ways followed till now by people who would move toward the Divine. You are going to cry that we are pretentious. Must we not suffer in imitation of the Saviour, while doing a little good around us ?

Vegetarian diet. — You may begin by observing ten monthly days. We abandon the flesh diet, because we would shun to bring suffering to beings that, though less evolved than we, yet know how to suffer as we. Medically speaking, man, because of his constitution, is not created to feed on flesh which his digestive organ ill supports. Besides, animals are ill as we, it is difficult to perceive it and men feed on sick parts. Man's sickness added to the animals', creates others, the nature of which medical science still is impotent to discover, still more impotent to heal.

The vegetarian diet generally brings a sweetness to man, always sound in body and spirit.

Since it is a matter of habit, we only ask new adherents for six days per month.

Altar.— Yes, you ought to have an altar. All you said in your letter is the exact truth. You must always share in the divine communion of ideas to the full, and the altar is there to remind you. A common prayer at a fixed time really puts the spirit of every one of us in the community of thought and gives a reflex in the divine astral that our Master (God) leads. Did not Christ say, that where two of you shall agree in prayer, your plea shall be heard ? We then may put ourselves in spirit under the eternal paternity of God.

The European, more than the Asiatic, must always have an altar in his house. In fact, he must work more than an Asiatic, for life is more difficult, and he must struggle from morning to evening for his daily bread. And his altar is there to remind him of his duties toward his Creator, when he comes home.

We must avoid numerous rites that smell of charlatanism or heresy ; but we must not radically do away with them. Intellectuals and scholars are generally brought to extremes ; they are either atheists or believers to the point of intolerance not to say fanatism. Let us be of the « golden mean » as the Sage Confucius recommends. In case of death, gather as many as possible of our Caodaist brethren for common prayers. These prayers are intended to facilitate the disincarnation of the dead and, by the force of concentrated thoughts, we lift the spirit of the dead toward superior planes which he alone cannot reach by his own efforts.

As for you, think of living long enough to propagate the new Faith, for the glory of our Divine Master. For us who know the death here-below is but the resurrection in the Beyond, death does not make us afraid ; it is to us, on the contrary, a deliverance. Yet, while we still may do a little material and moral good around us, we still must live long enough to fulfil the mission incumbent upon us. We only may progress and approach Divinity by a moral perfection of the soul, which is manifested by acts of charity and love. These are the only that empower us to enter into God's apanage.

Dignitaries. — God's universal government consists of two distinct branches : the one is a government of souls and beings and the other, instruction and education.

Most founders of religions belong only to the second branch : Branch of instructors. They are great legislators of God in this world. As God does not desire that, on earth, one man should hold all divine power, he divides it into two and commits it to two highest dignitaries.

I. — The Giáo-Tông holds the power and is the Chief of Cửu-Trùng-Đài ; Cửu : nine ; Trùng : planes ; Đài : palace (nine degrees of the angelic or divine Hierarchy and symbol of nine divine planes).

II. — The Hộ-Pháp is in charge of religious justice and looks after the application of law, and is the Chief of Hiệp-Thiên-Đài (place of meeting between God and Humanity). — Hiệp : union ; Thiên : God ; God united with men or men united with God.

I. — The former is attended by dignitaries enumerated in the pamphlet *Le Caodaisme ou Bouddhisme Rénové*, pages 35 and next in the chapter « Notre code religieux ».

The dignitaries of the « Confucianist » Branch (Ngọc, Vietnamese name) wear a purple gown which signifies « authority ».

Those of the « Buddhist » Branch (Thái) wear a « saffron yellow » gown (symbol of virtue).

Those of the « Taoist » Branch (Thượng) dresss in azure, symbol of Tolerance or Pacifism.

Only the Giáo-Tông and the Chưởng-Pháp of the « Taoist » Branch dress in white.

Lady-dignitaries also dress in white.

Dignitaries of the same grade, either Confucianists, or Taoists, or Buddhists have the same attributes, which are defined in the above-mentioned « Religious Code ». They are distinguished only by the colour of their costume.

When one of them is alone in a parish, he is the chief there, must see to everything and know everything. But when they are many in the same parish, the Superior of that parish may entrust them with the following works, based on their aptitudes, knowledges or on the branches to which they belong :

The Reds (Confucianists) may take charge of personnel, rites and order.

The Blues (Taoists) take care of the interior organization, office-works, instruction, education of the faithful, and charitable institutions.

The Yellows (Buddhists) see to finances, building, works, and various exchanges.

II. — The Hộ-Pháp is attended by the two following collaborators :

The Thượng-Phẩm who leads souls toward Nirvana.

The Thượng-Sanh who looks after men and brings them toward the Đạo (the Way and the Truth).

Each of these three great dignitaries has four immediate collaborators of the following branches (a little detailed explanation) :

The « Pháp » Branch (mysticism) has as a Chief the Hộ-Pháp who manages:

— The Bảo-Pháp, protector of established laws (mystic side)

— The Hiến-Pháp, he who seeks the Beautiful, the Good for the improving of what exists ;

— The Khai-Pháp, propagator ;

— The Tiếp-Pháp, he who helps in the application of laws and receives all complaints or suggestions.

The « Đạo » Branch (religious life) has as a Chief the Thượng-Phẩm who looks after :

The Bảo-Đạo, Hiến-Đạo, Khai-Đạo, Tiếp-Dạo, (same prerogatives as above, but in their branch).

The « Thế » Branch (social life) has as a Chief the Thượng-Sanh who sees to :
The Bảo-Thế, Hiến-Thế, Khai-Thế, Tiếp-Thế (same prerogatives as above, but in their branch).

These fifteen dignitaries form a Counsel having the right of jurisdiction and control. They communicate with God and Spirits as mediums.

They are seconded by a body of twelve academicians only some of which have been named.

To accede to these grades, one must begin by being: Archivist-secretary, then Registrar, Commissar of Justice, Lawyer, Inspector, Chancellor and Instructor.

When an Instructor has converted a nation, he may, according to vacancies, successively accede to one of the grades Tiếp, then Khai, afterwards Hiến, next Bảo, and to one of the three above-mentioned highest dignities. According also to his previous acquisitions, he shall be in one of the Three Branches Pháp, Dạo or Thế.

The High Dignitaries of « Hiệp-Thiên-Dài » are charged with the instruction and education of humanity, religious justice and control of the acts of those of Cửu-trùng-Dài, without, however, being able to interfere themselves in the government and administration of the sacerdocy. They are legislators. They also have a mission to propagate the new Faith by every means : press, meetings, etc. and to take care of the improvement and progress of Letters, Arts and everything that shall serve to help humanity to live with less suffering and in moral well-being.

I am of the « Taoist » Branch, as are a great number of dignitaries of the Foreign Mission, who are Spirits of Bạch-vân-Động (of the White Lodge) presently reincarnated to work for the success of the third Amnesty of God in the Orient.

The aura of each of us, according to the Divine Plane to which he belongs, has a particular coloration : blue, yellow, red or serene white. The Branch of each of us maybe revealed only by Guide-Spirits or our Divine Master, from our entry as members of the Sacerdocy, that is to say as dignitaries, beginning with Lễ-Sanh (student-priest).

Hymns. — As for hymns, we have them only in Vietnamese. There are prayers that date back to 1.200 years ago which Hàn-sơn-tự lamas (Hàn-sơn's pagoda) at Cô-Tô-Thành (Cô-Tô city) obtained in spiritist seances. Their translation is impossible to us at present. We shall later ask the spirists' help for European prayers. Very probably, Victor Hugo's spirit or Saint Joan of Arc will come for that purpose. I shall not fail to send them to you if need be. These few counsels should be sufficient to prove — once more — that Caodaism does not speak only to illiterate amorphous masses, for which life is a kind of animal half-sleep, but also to evolved and uplifted minds, with mystic tendencies who need intense religious satisfaction.

God's Altar and Offerings

God's Altar. — The Altar resembles a small house closed on three sides, the front being open, we put there a curtain. In time of prayer, we pull the curtain to expose a religious emblem (divine conscience), we light a pair of candles, five sticks of incense and sandal-wood (symbol of the five constitutive elements of man in a state of purification (complete sanctification of the being).

In private houses. — God's Altar may also be installed above the chimney of the sitting-room by furnishing it with objects of worship, without being in need of the small house described above.

Go'ds Altar may also be installed on a table, higher than ordinary tables, set against the wall in the room of honour of the house.

Hours. — Prayers are said four times a day.
1) between 5 and 7 o'clock a.m.
2) » 11 a.m. and 1 p.m.
3) » 5 and 7 p.m.
4) » 11 p.m. and 1 a.m.

Offerings. — We offer tea in the morning and evening, wine at noon and midnight. The tea is offered in a cup set beside another cup containing pure water; as for the wine, we put it in three liquor glasses. Cups and glasses must be covered when not in use.

On the first and fifteenth day of the lunar month and on feast-days, we offer flowers and fruits.

In the middle of the table of God's Altar, we put a small night-light that must be lit day and night for the flame represents the divine fire or divine light illuminating the Universe.

In time of prayer, we light two candles and five sticks of incense. We burn only sandal-wood in the great ceremonies.

Signification of the disposition of offerings. — We are taught in Bạch-ngọc-kinh (Nirvana) that our Supreme Master's throne is in the North, the rising is on the left, and the setting on the right.

It follows from this teaching that wherever God's Altar is installed, the divine Eye is in the North, then the rising or « dương » is on the left and the setting or « âm » is on the right.

In the Universe, there are two principles « âm » and « dương » that form the origin of all creation.

1.— The two candles symbolize the two masculine and feminine Logos united for production in general; the lunar and solar light (âm dương) still conserves the image of that productive power.

The left candle representing the solar light (dương) must be lit first.

2. — The five sticks of incense represent the five senses of man.

3. — The three glasses of wine represent the astral being or our vital energy. Wine is the true essence of vine as vitality is the essence of being. Vine and grape represent matter or our material body. Grape juice represents our vital energy or our astral. Wine is the spirit of the vine and the grape, it then symbolizes the divine spirit of our being or soul.

4. — The cup of pure water that symbolizes the «dương» must be put on the left of the divine Eye and the cup of tea that symbolizes the «âm» must be put on the right. (this tea and water is put together and forms holy water (âm dương). The holy water may be given as a drink to sick persons who have made earnest prayers, and received baptism)

Flowers representing the «dương» must be put on the left and fruits the «âm» on the right.

The infusion of those dry flowers, well preserved and transformed into decoction, can heal the sick who sincerely believe in the miracles of the Creator.

The three essential elements (Tam Tài) of the Universe are Heaven (Thiên), Earth (Địa), and Humanity (Nhơn). The Heaven is essentially constituted by the Sun (Nhựt), the Moon (Nguyệt) and the Stars (Tinh).

The Earth is essentially constituted by water (Thủy), fire (Hỏa) and ether (Phong).

Man is essentially constituted by matter (Tinh), the vital essence (Khí), the soul (Thần),

Offerings represent the three essential elements of our constitution. Flowers represent matter, wine, the vital energy and tea, the soul.

Rites and prayers

Before broaching the subject of rites, I must give you the explanation of «lạy».

In our country, «lạys» are exterior marks of veneration which we inwardly manifest to God, Superior Spirits, Sovereigns, the dead and our parents. They are, then, by no means humiliating, as some think. To make «lạys», we first begin by clasping the hands (mark of absolute confidence) in the following way.

We put the thumb of the left hand on the bottom of the ring-finger and we close the hand. We cover the left hand with the right by putting the thumb of the right hand on the bottom of the index-finger of the left hand.

Explanation of the position of both hands so joined. — The Heaven was created in the year Tý and Humanity in the year Dần, that is why we put the thumb of the left hand at the place of the year « Tý », and that of the right hand at the place of the year « Dần ».

In a standing position, we put the joined hands at the middle of the breast. Before prostrating ourselves, we bow deeply three times making an up and down movement with both arms forming a circle (the hands still joined) as a token of the offering of our ardent hearts to God.

To make « lays », one kneels, bringing the joined hands up to the forehead, lowering the open hands to the floor with crossed thumbs, and making « lays » by striking the head on both hands a certain number of times according to the grade of the Spirit to which the « lays » are made.

At the appointed time for public prayers, the faithful gathered in a room reserved for worship. They line up standing in two rows all along the room, the hands joined and laid on the breast ; priests in costume of ceremony in the first row ; men place themselves on the left, women on the right, at first face to face. As soon as everything is ready, they put themselves in a respectful position. Men and women salute one another by an inclination of the head and by the up and down motion with both arms widened into a circle, the hands joined. Then, groups of men and women move toward one another in such a way as to form rows of three or four persons or even more, according to the width of the room, being careful not to touch one another and leaving a free space in the middle, distinctly separating men from women, then they turn toward the altar, their eyes looking fixedly at the Divine Eye, the priest and faithful bow deeply three times before the altar, then kneel ; move the left foot a little forward, then fold the right foot first, then the left.

Caodaist Holy See. — Visit of H. R. H. Prince Bửu-Lộc, Director of the Cabinet of (H.M. Bao-Đại) (in black robe).

Anniversary of the 61st birthday of H.H. Hộ-Pháp. Spectators among whom are Consuls and Diplomatic Representatives of Foreign Nations. We notice H. H. Hộ-Pháp seated in the center, in tunicle.

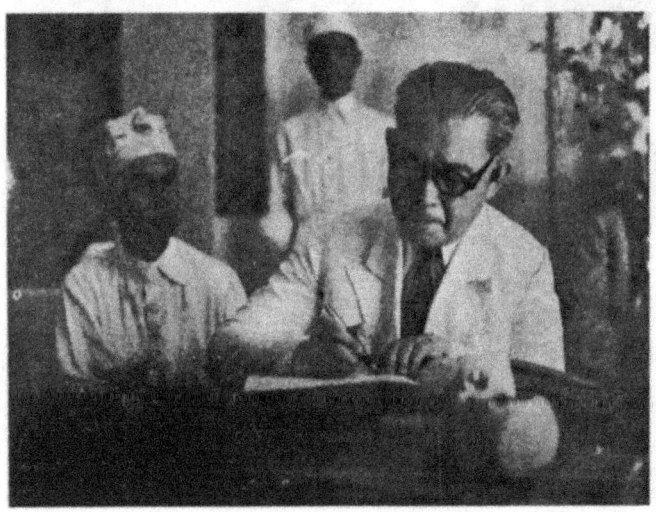

At the Residence of H. H. Hộ-Pháp. H. E. Trần-văn-Hữu, President of the Government of Vietnam, signing the Golden Book with his appreciation of the humanitarian aims of Caodaism.

At the Residence of H. H. Hộ-Pháp. Mr. Pignon, High Commissioner of France for Indochina, signing the Golden Book with his appreciation of the humanitarian aims of Caodaism.

At the Residence of H. H. Hộ-Pháp, General Chanson, Commanding the T.F.I.S., Commissioner of the Republic for South-Vietnam, signing the Golden Book with his appreciation of the humanitarian aims of Caodaism.

Interior of the Temple. — Before the Altar of Cao-Đài, high personalities meditate. In front : General Chanson (in uniform) Commanding the T.F.I.S., Commissioner of the Republic to South-Vietnam ;

At the center : H.E. Trần-văn-Hữu, President of the Government of Vietnam ; On the right : Mr. Pignon, High Commissioner of France for Indochina.

HISTORY AND PHILOSOPHY OF CAODAISM

They then make the following signs : first of all they bring both hands still joined up to the forehead, saying « Nam-Mô-Phật » (in Buddha's name) (related to God).

Afterwards, on the left, up to the ear, saying « Nam-mô-Pháp » (related to Nature).

Then, on the right, up to the ear, saying « Nam-mô-Tăng » (related to Humanity).

Then, on the breast, uttering the five sacramental invocations as follows :

1) Nam-Mô Cao-Dài Tiên-Ông Dại-Bồ-Tát Ma-ha-Tát (God) ;
2) Nam-Mô Quan-thế-Âm Bồ-Tát Ma-ha-Tát (Buddha) ;
3) Nam-Mô Lý-thái-Bạch Tiên-Trưởng (Taoism) ;
4) Nam-Mô Hiệp-Thiên Đại-Đế Quan-Thánh Đế-Quân ;
(Representatives of the three great religions : Confucianism, Taoism and Buddhism).
5) Nam-Mô chư Phật, chư Tiên, chư Thánh, chư Thần (Superior Spirits).

Make a deep bow after each invocation.

After each prayer, make three « lạys », that is to say to bow three times ; each time, touch the floor by your forehead : In prayer, a faithful asks his Divine Master to raise him in wisdom, to give him enough strength and courage to follow the Way (Dạo) traced by God and to give to Humanity the peace so often promised. A priest, besides his requests, prays to the Divine Master to protect him for propagating the Holy Doctrine, to teach him to know how to suffer that Humanity may leave in peace and to make universal peace reign.

The faithful must follow their priest with devotion in all his movements.

On feast-days, at the beginning of the ceremony, the officiating priest holds in his hands the five sticks of incense, while he makes the signs and utters the sacramental invocations ; afterwards he passes the sticks of incense to one of his assistants (standing near the altar). The latter plants them in a vase ad hoc.

At present, we have only prayers in Vietnamese. We pray to God in view of obtaining prayers in French. Meanwhile, the faithful make invocations and form vows :

At the end of the ceremony of worship, the assistants make « lays », stand up (always the right foot first), bow deeply before the altar three times, make a half-turn from right to left, turn toward Hộ-Pháp's altar (Buddha, Guardian of Nirvana) erected in front of the Divine Master's altar and pay reverence to him. Then, they come back to line up as at the beginning of the ceremony face to face and each one at his place.

They salute one another by a bow of the head and withdraw.

Hộ-Pháp's altar. — For the time being, one can place against the wall a little table on which we put a pair of candle-sticks, a vase for sticks of incense, a vase for sandal-wood, a glass for wine, a tea-cup, a water-cup, a flower-pot, a fruit-saucer. On the wall is hung a frame upon which are written these words : « Hộ-Pháp » (Buddha, Guardian of Nirvana, protector of the faithful) and the sign « Khí » or « Vital Breath » that resuscitates dying Humanity.

The Priests are careful, before the end of each great ceremony, to deliver a sermon exhorting the faithful to believe in God, the Creator and Common Father of all, to love one another, to gather souls for the Universal Peace.

Nota Bene. — As some are not accustomed to the « lạy », we can at present replace it by a deep reverence.

Signed : Thượng-Trung-Nhựt.

*
* *

This ritual may seem complicated to Occidentals, even those of good will, who may experience a certain revulsion in playing at choir boy. In its liberalism, in its spirit of tolerance, Caodaism allows great simplications, especially among certain European and American people not very demonstrative in matters of faith.

Furthermore, here is the extract of a Divine Message of the 18th of October 1936, a model of

A CAODAIST LIFE

Learn and practise my Doctrine according to the good Lord's rythm.

Do not encumber it with your own twaddle afterwards loading it with a thousand erasures ! (laughter)

Those who understood Holiness, shall know that my Law does not deliver to anybody his unfathomable Enigma.

∴

Live simply as the rest of mortals ;
But try to purify, in obscurity, the soul and the body.

My Doctrine does not impose upon you garments dyed in the bark of the già ;

Nor oblige you to shave your beard and hair, nor to abandon your family !

∴

While your parents and grand-parents live.
You must religiously pay your debt of filial Piety.
Spouses piously marry for life.
Keep that Holy Alliance pure as a Lotus that lives in mud and is not impregnated with its smell.

∴

Play wisely the Imbecile or the Idiot.
And do not display to others the Piety you keep at the bottom of your heart.

SPIRITUAL DIRECTIONS

(Extract of a letter)

There are a great many things that transcend the human understanding, that the human language is absolutely incapable to describe. So, the spirits who are manifested to us, have always recommended to us not to waste time in seeking to penetrate mysteries that they themselves are not in a position to unveil. Let us seek to know the Truth, which we need at present for our guidance, that we may not be in doubt ; once having found it, let us persevere in that way. In giving us this recommendation, the spirits do not intend to prevent us from seeking to know, to sound out mysteries, progressing day by day now, such is not their intention. They fear that we will waste our time looking for things that are not absolutely useful.

You may affirm to your friends that Khổng-Tử (or Kung-tze), Lão-tử (or Laotze), Gautama, Jesus of Nazareth, are but instructors, reflexes of the Cosmic mentality who is not a God distinctly separated from the Universe, but, on the contrary, strictly determined by it.

Each person, wicked, perverse though he may be, always possesses a little quality ; but nobody may pretend to be endowed with all qualities. God made us imperfect that we might have the consciousness of our weakness, in order to make us modest, to incite us to acquire more qualities, more virtues, to reach perfection. We must by our own means, progress, evolve more and more. Every one has what he needs to reach Divinity ; a Spirit may create a world which he shall be the Master of.

In my last letter, I explained to you the reason why we were led to forbid the faithful to dabble in communications with the Spirits by the means of un-official mediums. Notice that the formula of the oath dictated in the same spirit by our Divine Master also tends to make us aware of the manœuvres of ill spirits and that in dictating this formula, God knew that He was addressing followers who were in general Vietnamese, the majority of which, ignorant of Satan's temptations, should be easily seduced by him, which unfortunately has happened in recent years.

Christ had foretold Antichrist and the prediction was fulfilled. In Cochinchina, before and after the foundation of the new Doctrine, Antichrists had come and founded religious sects to sow division, to lead men astray from the way of Truth. They used all stratagems and found numerous victims.

As you see, the formula of the oath found its justification among us Vietnamese.

Hô-Phap and his insignia.
Hô : to protect ; Phap : law, rule, sign, symbol.

You distinguish three distinct objects that are Hô-Pháp's insignia: a) a kind of cube bearing the words « Xuân-Thu » ; b) a sort of cylinder ; c) a kind of stick having at one end a tuft of hair.

a) the cube represents a book consisting of five volumes called « Xuân-Thu » :

Xuân : Spring
Thu : Autumn

It is a social work written by Confucius in the form of a Gospel and which signifies moral perfection, teaching, besides rites, divination of oracles, literature, music and the rules of Humanity: «duties of man, citizen, father and mother, husband and wife, son, brother and sister, master and pupil, public official, sovereign, even duties toward animals and plants ».

It is the symbol of Confucianism. This book is called Xuân-Thu for Confucius' idea makes human morals sprout and fructify as the Spring and Autumn which are two seasons having days and nights of equal length and easy to bear.

b) the cylinder represents a big bowl, in which Buddha Shakyamuni in his days, was accustomed to receive food offered by his followers. Heir presumptive of the richest monarch, the mightiest kingdom of India, the prince Siddharta, later become the Buddha Shakyamuni, had the courage to leave all his worldly wealth to go and seek in solitude Peace of soul and heart and Truth. He had to beg for his living to nourish his body in view of propagating the Faith he had acquired,

The bowl is called « Bình-bát-du » :
Bình : basin
bát : bowl
du (pronounced You) : to beg.

(a bowl in the form of a basin to receive alms), is the symbol of detachment from the riches of this world, abnegation, renunciation, total disinterestedness of life (asceticism).

It is the insignia of Buddhism.

c) The stick ornamented with a tuft of hair is called Phất-chủ :
Phất : to move or drive
Chủ : dust.

or Phất-trần (drive impurities from this world) symbolizes the moral exercise that consists in purifying itself day by day from all faults. As its name indicates, Phất-Chủ is used to drive impurities from this world.

It is the symbol of Taoism, the symbol of purity of sentiment.

In short, the three doctrines : « Confucianism, Taoism, Buddhism » (Christianity being considered as one of the branches of Confucianism), are the three stages of the evolution of soul, the three degrees of initiation that bring the spirit toward pure divinity.

The three above-described objects united form Hộ-Pháp's insignia, for this dignitary, spiritually speaking, is entrusted with the responsibility of uniting the three doctrines and to see men live in peace and in respect of the laws of evolution.

The Thông-Sự, called Hộ-Pháp Em (Em : younger brother ; Hộ-Pháp's miniature), for he inherits from Hộ-Pháp a little part of his authority, that of rendering justice to his brethren of his hamlet, wears on his gown of ceremony, on the right and left of the breast, two badges (the three insignia put side by side) and on the turban, just at the middle of the forehead, the same badge.

The Phó-Trị-Sự is called Giáo-Tông Em (Giáo-Tông in miniature) because he represents in his hamlet the Giáo-Tông who personifies love toward all beings, who lovingly looks after every act of life of each member, the peace of his spirit and heart, the progress of his evolution. The Phó-trị-Sự wears a gown ornamented at the collar with a band of ribbon made of silver-white woven thread, and at the left arm a bit a tricoloured ribbon : yellow : Buddhism ; blue : Taoism ; red : Confucianism. This is the exterior reflection of the three doctrines.

The Chánh-Trị-Sự is called Dầu-Sư Em (Dầu : first, Sư : master, Em : younger brother) or first master of the younger brother, or the eldest in the village. The Dầu-Sư received two powers conferred by Giáo-Tông and Hộ-Pháp. The Chánh-Trị-Sự then fulfils Giáo-Tông and Hộ-Pháp's authorities in the village. He wears a white gown ornamented at the collar with a strip of ribbon made of golden-yellow woven thread and on the left arm a bit of tricoloured ribbon of a size larger than that of the Phó-Trị-Sự. He has on his turban Hộ-Pháp's insignia.

Our Holy See is now engaged in producing a translation of Pháp-Chánh-Truyền:

Pháp : Law, rule, sign, symbol, etc. everything that comes from the Law of evolution ;

Chánh : stable, infallible, inviolable, perfect correction (the golden mean of all) ;

Truyền : order, constitution :

Pháp-Chánh-Truyền : rules of the inviolable constitution.

The Author of these Rules is our Divine Master Cao-Dài who dictated them to us by mediumnic communications.

May we repeat : these explanations, though very summary, can yet appear very complicated for the Occidental who is frightened by the *minuteness* of detail, characteristic of Oriental worships. Let them be assured : here too, always, Caodaism admits great simplifications in certain countries.

As for children of European type of which you spoke to me in one of your letters, scoffers will say that they result from a crossing. But, by serious study, and observation, we are able to affirm that these children are born of honest mothers of Vietnamese families, having lived with Vietnamese husbands. They have never set foot in the towns inhabited and frequented by Europeans and have always lived in isolated corners which no European has visited. Yet, certain of their children have features of European or Aryan race ; they may sometimes have a European form, and gait, but their hair is always black like that of any other Vietnamese.

We believe we know that these children conserve a part of their physique from preceding reincarnations — where they were born from European parents. They are born most often under the astral they had in their preceding reincarnations.

By revelations, we confirmed that a man, having a split lip in a preceding reincarnation, actually bears a hare-lip ; that another who was an evolved animal, still conserves a part of his old instincts, of his previous physical constitution.

These things make a materialist smile naturally, who yet would fear to light three cigarettes (two friends and himself) by the same match, to drive without a mascot or a fetish, to lunch or dine in the number of thirteen, to cross the arms of friends in shaking hands at departure, etc...

The «unaccustomed» has always been the target of our sarcasms and repulsions, what a poor and weak man we are !

The Caodaist experience in Europe has provoked these conclusions from a brother in Cao-Dài :

« Certain formulas, certain external aspects of Caodaism should be modified in order to be able to keep effectively the attention of persons susceptible of taking it into consideration. I think — and this is already for me an experience — that the picture of the altar representing the symbolic and shining Eye, might be advantageously substituted for the very highly coloured images of divinities or avatars that appear in the believer's home.

Here, in France, people so much prefer simplicity, a sketch, great suggestive outlines, at least among the particular public to which I necessarily must address myself. I must say in this connection that the superb picture you sent me of Quan-Âm Bồ-Tát (Kwan-Yn) pleases enormously, and I believe I know the reason why it is very little coloured and simpler than that of the emblem or even that of Quan-Thánh Dế-Quân. I already wrote to you about rites and prayers that might be simplified to make place for simple meditation, perhaps interspersed with short invocations. I think that in France, people might make brief but substantial readings before the altar of Dạo : all this is a matter of comprehension, adaptation, tolerance. The lamp of the altar (Thái-Cực-Dăng) is another of the liturgical things that should be better understood and accepted : it goes without saying the most specially consecrated men, such as the dignitaries, could in practice take certain liberties, still conforming as much as possible to the symbolisms fo Vietnam.

Concerning doctrine or teaching, I have written you long and often, I shall come back to it only to affirm once more that it should be eminently preferable not to insist on the personal aspect of the Divinity, to which I attribute without hesitation all responsibility for the existing occidental materialism. People do not want any more of a Jehovah God with arbitrary decisions. All my requests for explanation and conversations I have had since December 1934 on the subject of Đạo are convergent and conclusive on that capital point : Kung-tze, Lao-tze, Gautama, Jesus of Nazareth are but instructors, reflections of the Cosmic mentality who is not a God distinctly separated from the Universe, but on the contrary, strictly determined by it. If I preach the contrary, people would listen to me but for politeness' sake or they would tell me to go back to Rome.

How delicate it is for me, and painful, my dearest and venerated Brother, to dilute that which I feel to be of vital importance for the diffusion of Đạo in France! I am brought to believe, after what you wrote me concerning my confidences, that my actual reincarnation in the Occident, at this time, is quite karmic, allowing me to make, in my modest circle a liaison between a world that is fallen and another that tends to the horizon.

But how many misunderstandings it has to meet here ! How many nuances to define to christian or materialistic ears, so similar in their dogmatisms issued from a common illusion (Samara) ! »

These just reflexions, that go back to 1935, have lost nothing of their value : experienced in the West, in France, Caodaism calls for a simplification for certain souls who live in a « voltairian climate » and who reject the formulas and too complicated rites of an Oriental theosophy : Let us add that this same complication, more apparent than real, is a powerful attraction, a suave delight for certain souls, avid for mysticism (in the most beautiful and noble meaning of the word).

CAODAISM AND ITS VARIOUS BRANCHES

The religious communion of Caodaism or Đại-Đạo Tam-Kỳ Phồ-Độ (3rd Amnesty of God in the Orient) receives its instructions and impulsions from TâyNinh's Holy See.

It was born in Cochinchina in 1926 and was officially declared by a letter of the late Lê-văn-Trung, former Colonial Counsellor, afterwards become Quyền-Giáo-Tông (temporary Pope : the titular being Saint Thái-Bạch's Spirit), to the Governor of Cochinchina, on the 7th of September.

The present Superior of the religion is the Hộ-Pháp Phạm-công-Tắc whose official Delegate at Saigon is the Phối-Sư Trần-quang-Vinh.

Some former high dignitaries of Tâyninh's Caodaism have left the communion and created separate sects, preserving the same name of Caodaism. Mr. Nguyễn-ngọc-Tương, ex-Phủ (Bếntre's sect) and Mr. Nguyễn-văn-Ca, ex-Đốc-Phủ (Mỹtho's sect).

Other have gone the same way and founded other sects.

At present (1948), there are 11 sects of the Caodaist communion. Being anxious for exactness and impartiality according to our brother Gago's spirit, here is the list of those sects and branches with the name of their chiefs and the headquarters of each :

Various sects of Caodaism

Serial number	Denomination of sects	Names of chiefs	Headquarters	Observations
1	Minh-Chơn-Lý	Nguyễn-văn-Ca	Mỹ-Tho	Mr. Tý gives himself the title of President of the Caodaist Union (deceased at Hải-Phòng in 1948)
2	Ban-Chỉnh-Đạo	Nguyễn-ngọc-Tương	Bến-Tre	
3	Tiên-Thiên	Lê-kim-Tỵ	Phú-Nhuận (Gia-Định)	
4	Thông-Thiên-Đài	Quách-Văn-Nghĩa and Lê-Quang-Hộ	Gò-Công Saigon	
5	Liên-Hòa Tổng-Phái	Nguyễn-Phan-Long and Trần-Văn-Quế	Cầu-Kho Saigon	
6	Minh-Chơn-Đạo or Công-Đồng Hội-Giáo	Cao-Triều-Phát	Bạc-Liêu	
7	Trung-Hoa Học-Phái	Trương-Kế-An	Thủ-Dầu-Một	Mr. An has opened a medical office at Thủ-Dầu-Một.
8	Tây-Tông (Vô-Cực)	Nguyễn-Bửu-Tài	Bến-Tre	Mr. Tài withdrew to TayNinh's Holy See where he resides.
9	Tuyệt-Cốc	Nhuận and Ruộng	Tay-Ninh	They are ascetics living secluded and very little known.
10	Chiêu-Minh-Đàn	Tư-Quỳnh	Cái-Khế (Cần-Thơ)	The late Đốc-Phủ Ngô-văn-Chiêu is its founder.
11	Nữ-Trung Hoa-Phái	Ngọc-Nhiên-Hương and Lê-Ngọc-Trinh	Saigon	

The principal characteristic of Caodaism is the worship of Cao-Dài Tiên-Ông Dại-Bồ-Tát Ma-Ha-Tát, the same God (Trời) worshipped by the five religious branches (chi) hereafter named under the name of Ngọc-Hoàng Thượng-Dế.

Here is the list of the five actual branches of Buddhism:

Denomination of « Chi »	Names of Chiefs	See of branches	Observations
Minh-Lý	O-Kích (Âu-Kích)	Saigon	Tam-Tông-Miếu Pagoda Rue Chasseloup-Laubat
Minh-Sư	Trần-Dạo-Quang	An-Nhơn (Gia-Dinh)	Linh-quang-Tự Pagoda
Minh-Tân	Lê-Minh-Khá	Vĩnh-Hội (Saigon)	The only « chi » having adhered to Caodaism exploited by the Caodaist Union.
Minh-Thiện	Dạt and Mùi	Thủ-Dầu-Một	Minh-Thiện Pagoda
Minh-Dường	Lê-văn-Lịch	Cần-Giộc (Chợ Lớn)	

Toward Union

In 1945, TâyNinh's Holy See took the initiative in working for the unification of all « chi » (branches) and all « phái » (sects). The former municipal counsellor of Chợ-Lớn, Mr. Nguyễn-hữu-Dắc, was entrusted with this mission. Mr. Dắc's attitude being appreciated as not conforming to the spirit that animated the Holy See, he publicly gave up his project. Mr. Dắc did not cease to pursue his conversations which ended in a meeting at the of Minh-Tân Pagoda at Vĩnh-Hội (Saigon). A committee was elected with Mr. Cao-triều-Phát of Bắc-Liêu as President and Mr. Lê-Kim-Ty as vice-President.

At this « Caodaist Union » (Cao-Dài Hiệp-nhứt), the orthodox Communion of TâyNinh and most of other sects, especially those of Bến-tre and Mỹ-tho did not participate.

In September 1946, Mr. Lê-Kim-Ty, vice-president tried vainly to convene a general assembly of sects, first at the pagoda of Minh-Tân at Vĩnh-Hội, then at Mr. Nguyễn-ngọc-Thơ's Bạch Vân-Am temple at Phú-Lâm (Chợ-Lớn), the proprietors of these pagodas not having accepted the responsibilities of fact and intention of the promoter of the meeting.

At last, Mr. Lê-Kim-Ty took advantage of a worship ceremony at the home of ex-adjutant Bùi-văn-Nhàn at Phú-Nhuận on the occasion of the 15th day of the 8th month (September 10th) to have acclaimed President of the Caodaist Union by a group of followers of Tiên-Thiên to which were joined some members of other sects unauthorized by their sacerdocy. Mr. Nhàn was promoted vice-president.

Tây-Ninh's Orthodox Caodaism has no relation with « the Caodaist Union » above-mentioned.

It is good to draw attention to these various tendencies precisely to avoid confusion and to lead all those who wish for Union, for Synthesis, for Communion toward its true and only actual point of Caodaist radiance, His Holiness Phạm-Công-Tắc, Hộ-Pháp at TâyNinh, and toward his active Delegate at Saigon : His Eminence Trần-quang-Vinh, Phối-Sư.

Here is an outline on the Organization and Hierarchy of Caodaism.

a) *Holy See*

The Holy See is situated at TâyNinh, four kilometers from the town. We find there a great Temple that is the work of modern Sino-Vietnamese religious architecture conceived and realized by His Holiness Phạm-công-Tắc himself, the size of which is comparable to that of European Cathedrals.

Important religious services are installed there as well as agricultural, forest and industrial (saw-mill, brick-yard, etc.) works.

It is a holy city equipped with a school, a hospital, a market, a playing-field, broad, clean and well-maintained streets.

At present, numerous crews of workmen of various specialities work feverishly at equipping and town-planning.

The inner enclosure is protected by a semi-military armed guard, who are preparing recruits destined for self-defence posts in the provinces.

The Holy See houses a population of more than 10,000 persons. Outside the enclosure, there is an agglomeration of followers estimated at more than 80,000 inhabitants.

The Religion's Direction comprises :

I.— The Cửu-Trùng-Dài or Executive Body which represents the Temporal Power ;

II.— The Hiệp-Thiên-Dài or Legislative Body which represents the Spiritual Power. From an esoterical point of view, this Body holds the mystic power.

III.— The Cơ-Quan Phước-Thiện or Works of Charity.

I. — CỬU-TRÙNG-ĐÀI

At the head of Cửu-Trùng-Dài, is enthroned the Giáo-Tông (Pope) whose titular is Saint Lý-Thái-Bạch's Spirit. Since the creation of the religion, the late Lê-văn-Trung is the only human being who received the title of Quyền-Giáo-Tông (Temporary Pope) and was the true Chief of the Religion. He has not yet his successor. Wanting the Giáo-Tông, the Hộ-Pháp, Chief of Hiệp-Thiên-Đài, became Superior of Caodaism.

The hierarchy of the dignitaries of Cửu-Trùng-Đài is schematically established in the following fashion :

SERIAL NUMBER	TITLE	ENGLISH EQUIVALENT TITLE	NUMBER APPOINTED	OBSERVATIONS
1	Giáo-Tông	Pope	1 titular	vacant
2	Chưởng-Pháp	Censor Cardinal	3 titulars	vacant
3	Đầu-Sư	Cardinal	3 titulars	vacant
4	Chánh-Phối-Sư	Principal Archbishop	3 titulars	vacant
5	Phối-Sư	Principal Archbishop	33 titulars	insufficient
6	Giáo-Sư	Bishop	72 titulars	insufficient
7	Giáo-Hữu	Priest	3,000 titulars	
8	Lễ-Sanh	Student-Priest	unlimited number	
9	Chánh-Trị-Sự	Lesser dignitary	unlimited number	
10	Phó-Trị-Sự	Lesser dignitary	unlimited number	
11	Thông-Sự	Lesser dignitary	unlimited number	
12	Tín-Đồ	follower		

For the Administration of the Religion, the Cửu-trùng-Đài comprises 9 religious Ministries or « Viện » :

1. — Lại-Viện............... Interior
2. — Lễ-Viện............... Rites
3. — Hòa-Viện............... Security
4. — Hộ-Viện............... Finances
5. — Lương-Viện............ Supply
6. — Học-Viện............... Education
7. — Nông-Viện............. Agriculture
8. — Công-Viện............. Public Works
9. — Y-Viện............... Health.

SERIAL NUMBER	TITLE	ENGLISH EQUIVALENT TITLE	EQUIVALENT TITLE IN THE CỬU-TRÙNG-ĐÀI	OBSERVATIONS
1	Hộ-Pháp	Holder of religious laws and rules, Master of the Mystic Branch.	Pope	The Superior
2	Thượng-Phẩm	Chief of the Sacerdotal Body (Defender and Protector of the Sacerdocy)	Censor Cardinal	Deceased, not replaced
3	Thượng-Sanh	Chief of all the lesser order of the Religion from simple followers to Lễ-sanh.	Censor Cardinal	
4	Tiếp-Pháp			
5	Tiếp-Đạo	Legislator	Cardinal	
6	Tiếp-Thế			
7	Khai-Pháp			
8	Khai-Đạo	Reformer	Cardinal	
9	Khai-Thế			
10	Hiến-Pháp			
11	Hiến-Đạo	Renovator	Cardinal	
12	Hiến-Thế			
13	Bảo-Pháp			
14	Bảo-Đạo	Conservator	Cardinal	
15	Bảo-Thế			

The Secondary Cadre of Hiệp-Thiên-Đài comprises the following dignitaries :

SERIAL NUMBER	TITLE	ENGLISH EQUIVALENT TITLE	EQUIVALENT TITLE IN THE CỬU-TRÙNG-ĐÀI	OBSERVATIONS
1	Tiếp-Dẫn-Đạo Nhơn	Instructor	Principal Archbishop	
2	Chưởng-Ấn	Chancellor	Archbishop	
3	Giám-Đạo	General Inspector	Principal Archbishop	
4	Cải-Án	Lawyer	Bishop	
5	Thừa-Sử	Historian	Priest	
6	Truyền-Trạng	Investigator	Priest	
7	Sĩ-Tải	Archivist	Student-Priest	
8	Luật-Sư	Master of Doctrine	Sub-dignitary	

II. — HIỆP-THIÊN-ĐÀI

At the head of Hiệp-Thiên-Đài is placed the Hộ-Pháp (Grand Chief of the Legislative Body) assisted by a Thượng Phẩm and a Thượng-Sanh.

These three high dignitaries command the Thập-nhị Thời-Quân (12 members of the Legislative Body).

The hierarchy of the dignitaries of Hiệp-Thiên-Đài is established, according to the divine instruction, in the following way: (see table opposite).

III. — CƠ-QUAN PHƯỚC-THIỆN

The Cơ-Quan Phước-Thiện (Charitable Body) mainly looks after the aged, widows, orphans, in short all the underprivileged, whether they belong to Caodaism or not. They morally and materially support the families of dignitaries who have vowed to abandon their homes to consecrate themselves entirely to Religion.

To reach that aim, it is important that this organism have at its disposal necessary financial and material means. For this purpose, the Charitable Body received the authorization of the Sacerdotal Body to set itself to forest and industrial works, to the development of rice and food cultivation, to the breeding of cattle and pigs, and even to activities of local commerce. The gratuitous help of the voluntary members of the Charitable Body is utilized according to their competence and skills.

List of the Caodaist Charitable Body

TITLE	EQUIVALENT TITLE IN THE CƯU-TRÙNG-ĐÀI
Phật-Tử	Pope
Tiên-Tử	Censor Cardinal
Thánh-Nhơn	Cardinal
Hiền-Nhơn	Principal Archbishop
Đạo-Nhơn	Archbishop
Chơn-Nhơn	Bishop
Chí-Thiện	Priest
Giáo-Thiện	Student-Priest
Hành-Thiện	Sub-dignitary
Thính-Thiện	Earnest Faithful
Tân-Dân	Earnest Faithful
Minh-Đức	Simple Member

At present, the dignitaries of the highest rank of the Charitable Body reach only the rank of « Chí-Thiện » (Priest).

b) *In the provinces*

For practical reasons, Caodaism has adopted as religious circumscriptions, existing administrative divisions in Cochinchina.

It comprises five « Trấn » led by Khâm-Trấn-Đạo who are chosen among the dignitaries having the rank of Giáo-Sư (Bishop).

Each province has at its head a Khâm-Châu-Đạo who ranks among the Giáo-Hữu (Priest).

The Đầu-Tộc-Đạo administers an area corresponding to a government administrative delegation. He is chosen among the Lễ-Sanh (Student-Priest).

The Đầu-Hương-Đạo, chief of a village parish, ranks among the Chánh-Trị-Sự (lesser dignitary).

In hamlets, there are Phó-Trị-Sự or Tri-Lý-Đạo and Thông-Sự or Thông-Lý-Đạo (lesser dignitaries).

The provincial dignitaries hold their see either in Văn-Phòng (offices) especially organized for that purpose or in meeting-places where they install their offices.

CAODAISM
State Religion, National Religion of Vietnam

A document of 1946
Caodaism : its origin, character, projects

Caodaism is of a spiritual essence. Its creation proceeds from spiritism. Its doctrine and worship were taught to men by the interpreter of the billed-basket. Messages came either from the Supreme God, Cao-Dài Himself, or Superior Spirits such as Lý-Thái-Bạch, the Chinese Poet Ly-Tai-Pé of the Đường (Tang) dynasty, now become spiritual Pope of Caodaism. Spirits of European great men among others Victor Hugo (Nguyệt-Tàm Chơn-Nhơn) often intervened to dictate religious precepts in verse.

Caodaism is an amalgam, a synthesis of existing religions : Confucianism, Taoism, Buddhism, Christianity, etc. — It does not neglect animistic worships and the deification of heroes of the Sino-Vietnamese antiquity.

The architecture of the Đền-Thánh (Great Temple) which draws the admiration of foreign tourists by its audacious conception and scope, was inspired by the Pope Lý-Thái-Bạch or Hộ-Pháp Phạm-công-Tắc, present Superior of Caodaism, who had the merit of accomplishing the building with very reduced means under the most unfavourable circumstances. It is artistically decorated with all the symbols of the associated religions, legends and beliefs of the Sino-Vietnamese folklore : This heterogeneous mixture makes of it a monument of great originality. The most characteristic of innovations, is the Tower of Saker (Nghinh-Phong) from where melodious and enchanting modulations of an invisible chorus mysteriously escape. It is crowned with a fabulous animal, the Dragon-Horse (Long-Mã) that carries on its back the first signs of the Chinese Zodiac.

The worship has its peculiarities. Prostrations are made not with joined flat hands, but with hands so joined as to form a ball, both thumbs being hidden inside. Instead of three traditional sticks of incense, five are burned at each ceremony. Offerings of flowers, tea and alcohol are made on an altar where the Oriental Gods are close to Jesus Christ. The religious emblem is the divine Eye darting its beams on a cosmic globe. This is the eternal light.

The administrative structure is that of a modern State. There are the Executive Power (Cửu-trùng-Đài) the Legislative Power (Hiệp-Thiên-Đài) and the Charitable Body (Cơ-Quan Phước-Thiện), distinctive token of the religion.

The Cửu-Trùng-Đài or Executive Power is divided into three branches (Phái) :

Thượng or Taoism, symbol : azure.

Ngọc or Confucianism, symbol : red.

Thái or Buddhism, symbol : yellow.

These three colours form the tricoloured banner of Caodaism.

The Caodaist regime is fundamentally democratic. Nominations and promotions in the episcopal hierarchy are first submitted to an assembly of Faithful (Vạn-Linh) composed of representatives of parishes in the ratio of one delegate per 500 members or fraction thereof. They are then submitted to the Sacerdotal Counsel, the High Counsel, and finally, the Spiritual Pope Lý-Giáo-Tông.

The Holy See is situated at TâyNinh, 4 kilometers from the chief-town of the province.

It is a town having an area of 100 hectares, equipped with modern installations, printing-house, police-station, play-ground, weaving-mill and furniture-factory, administrative offices and also an undertaking-service. It has its brickyard, sawmill, and public-works. Its kitchens and refectories are of considerable size.

Caodaism has seen 22 years of existence (in 1948). It might take on more breadth. It is busy with its works of reconstruction and arrangement.

It knew its hard beginnings. The persecutions were due to a want of understanding on the part of some, and the evil intent of others.

Interior dissensions gave birth to eleven dissident sects.

The war was a hard blow for Caodaism. The five-year absence of the Superior Phạm-Công-Tắc, exiled from 1941 to 1946 to Madagascar with five of his dignitaries, deprived it of its most dynamic animators.

The demolition of buildings and other unavoidable consequences of military operations, are hard felt.

There remain of the archives and the old library only valueless documents.

The projected monastery remains in the blue-print stage.

All now must be reconstituted, reconstructed, re-begun.

To a religion, time does not matter.

Relying on its faith and divine protection, Caodaism continues its way, softly but certainly, to accomplish the Celestial Mission.

Future projects :

It does not lack ambitions in the domain of realizable projects :

« To make of Caodaism a religion of State, the national religion of Vietnam ;

« To make of the Caodaist Holy See a center of pilgrimage and tourism, not only for Vietnam and its neighbouring countries, but also and especially for the far nations of Europe and America ;

« To extend proselytism in the world and have, at least in the great capitals, meeting-places where Caodaist missionaries shall come preaching the Love of Neighbour and Universal Brotherhood ».

To realize these dreams, Caodaism knows that it counts on the sponsorship of the new France, a Great Friend and a Good Counsellor.

Saigon, November 10th, 1946.
Trần-quang-Vinh

His Excellency Trần-Quang-Vinh,
Major-general, Commander-in-Chief
of the Caodaist Troops,
Minister of the Armed Forces
of the Government of Vietnam.

WHAT HIS EXCELLENCY TRẦN-QUANG-VINH THINKS ABOUT REINCARNATION BY CAODAISM

The Law of reincarnation, when one seeks to the sources of Wisdom, is at the origin of all religions. Every searcher of truth in the Orient or Occident, every truly religious person, without distinction of belief, must conceive and recognize that that law is unique from an esoteric point of view and shall always remain so ; whence the certitude of the immortality of the soul and the evolution of each being after successive existences.

Caodaism or Reformed Buddhism, in order to realize religious unity, takes into consideration the pure principles acknowleged as being eternal truths of the Four Great Religions and practises the broadest tolerance toward all forms of Faith, however reserving for itself to bring them back, by persuasion, to the original Unity.

Now, our doctrine is founded by Spiritism, on the teaching of our Divine Master, it is natural that we should conceive of the Reincarnation, in the manner of spiritualists of India and the Occident and take as a fundamental Axis the karmic Law that was taught of old the secret seal in the temples of India, Chaldees and Egypt. It is simple, comprehensible, because for common people and learned persons, truth does not change its form. As the sun that shines for all over the world, the divine Law is applied to all the Universe and even imposed upon vegetation and the beasts.

Is it not the goal of every religious man to reach the Wisdom of the Soul ? Is it not the eternal Glory of all spirits to acquire the riches of God's virtue and be rendered immortal. The result is learning to know oneself first, and then knowing, by conscience, *the Being who must be*. To reach this supreme aim, from unclean matter to pure Divinity, all vitality, all energy, all being, makes its way tramping through numerous reincarnations. Now, who says Reincarnation says Suffering, who says Suffering says Love. Christ, Buddha, Laotze and Confucius did not step aside from that way. The Truth taught by our Divine Master and conceived by each of those instructors of Humanity is always one.

They who pretend otherwise are far from Truth. They are persons rushing to enjoy a beatitude and perfect rest after the hard terrestrial trial and who would pass in one bound from our planet to the Seventh Heaven and Nirvana. To those eager for easy Paradises, we must recall that great occultists as well as great philosophers who have affirmed successive lives, believed that the soul, arrived at perfection, ceases to be reincarnated to live a life of Cosmic transcendence. But to reach perfection of the soul is a long journey. The number of stages depends on each spirit. Meanwhile, successive lives are necessary for the extension of sensibility, the development of intelligence and the exercise of will. This theory is the only one that gives a plausible explanation of the evolution of the soul by uniting it to the Law of Reincarnation.

Such is the Law of strict justice proving the real and infinite kindness of God. His Creatures are responsible only for their actions and the conscience is a severe judge who marks each suffering with a step taken toward evolution.

From the preceding statement, it is easy to understand that the reincarnated being does not wholly differ from the terrestrial being, which we might know. Little by little, as it accumulates existences, the spirit creates an individuality that is permanent, constantly keeps on improving it, whatever may be the different bodies that it momentarily animates later to be abandoned. The progress of the spirit or the soul increases according to the merit of each life, but the evolution does not prevent the soul, in certain cases, from spontaneously remembering his past lives. Mr. Léon Denis has, on the problem of being and Destiny, given precious indications and God has granted them to give the world proof of the reality of successive existences.

In his Treatise on Egyptian Mystic, Jambique expresses the following :

God's Justice is not the Justice of men. Man defines Justice in relation to his actual life and his present state. God defines it relatively to our successive lives and to the universality of our lives. Thus the pains that afflict us are often punishments for sin which the soul has committed in a previous life.

They who pretend the contrary ill understand the divine Justice. As Allan Kardec so justly wrote : we must be born and reborn and ceaselessly progress. Knowledge of this law will enable men to destroy utterly within themselves all selfishness, hate, envy and pride. It will teach to all the acceptance of suffering for the perfection of the soul and help those who suffer to understand the reasons for inequalities herebelow. By placing the divine above the human, it puts at the Zenith of the Cosmos the key to all problems.

ESSENTIAL ELEMENTS OF CAODAISM

According to the teachings of the Supreme Being, the Doctrines of the various religions through the centuries have been denatured and badly practised even by those who were charged with spreading them. The order and peace of the days of old are effaced, the moral Law of Humanity is quite betrayed, the world is at present in darkness. A new religion is needed, capable of maintaining humanity in the love of creation and fraternization of all races. The Caodaist Doctrine sets itself this heavy task. To the eternal truths, to the divine Law, Caodaism conforms its dogmas and principles. It respects others' beliefs when those beliefs are not of a nature to lead humanity to Fanatism or Heresy. Where certain truths are deformed by superstitious conceptions of ignorance, the new religion undertakes to re-establish them in their true meaning. The scheme of our great way tends not only to conciliate all religious convictions, but also to adapt itself to all degrees of spiritual evolution.

From a moral point of view, our Doctrine reminds man of his duties toward himself, his family, society, which is a wider family, and finally humanity, the universal family.

From a philosophical point of view, it preaches disinterestedness toward honours, riches, luxury, in a word, a freeing from the servitude of matter to seek in spirituality, the full quietude of the soul.

From the point of view of worship, it recommends the adoration of God, the Father of All, the veneration of Superior Spirits who constitute the August Occult Hierarchy and the Founders of great Religions, true instructors of Humanity.

From a spiritualistic point of view, it confirms, in harmony with other religions and with the systems of spiritualistic and psychical philosophy, the existence of the soul, its survival of the physical body, its evolution by the plurality of existence, the posthumous consequences of human action ordered by the karmic Law.

From the point of view of the initiate, it communicates to those of the dignitaries who are worthy, revealed teachings that shall empower them, by a process of spiritual evolution, to accede to ravishments of beatitude.

∴

To evangelize the world and unite all the Master's children, we, his disciples, have only to draw our force and wisdom from his divine teachings. His doctrine is a reformed doctrine, the only one capable of bringing back universal Peace drawn from the fusion of the principal religions of the Orient and of Christianity, and actually spread over much of the terrestrial globe under different forms. With him, we shall dissipate everything that is of error and pretention, overthrow all obstacles and everywhere sow Wisdom and Love.

The spotless Truth can come only from Him, for all human bodies are subject to error, and no one herebelow can penetrate His secrets.

He is the true Father and Master of Humanity because it is from Him that comes all our being. Father, He gives us Vitality ; Master, He bequeaths us his own Divinity.

Note. — The Buddhist Truth on the karmic Law is always the same Gautama Buddha said :

« The Present is the Result of the Past which was our Work.

« The Future shall bring forth an effect of which the Present is the cause ».

Saigon, November 10th, 1946.
The Delegate of the Superior of Caodaism :
Trần-quang-Vinh.

SOME WORDS FROM THE HOLY SEE

The newspaper *le Khmer* (30-5-37) briefly interviewed His Holiness Phạm-Công-Tắc, present Superior of Caodaism. Here is the text of the interview:

« We shall not undertake to revive, in these lines, the show and splendor of the ceremonies marking the inauguration of the Caodaist temple of PhnomPenh, our colleagues having done it so well.

We only aim at examining with our readers, with all impartiality, the declarations that His Holiness Phạm-Công-Tắc, Supreme Chief of the Caodaist Religion, so kindly gave us.

We were profoundly moved and touched at the welcome we received from this man, by his modesty and by his great simplicity! Our conversation was cordial, friendly, we might say fraternal, for at no time did His Holiness Phạm-Công-Tắc try to pontificate, nor give proof of the least intolerance.

He is a very enlightened man. His religious conceptions are no doubt somewhat different from ours, but the ideal pursued is so beautiful, that we could only bow before his sincere faith, reminding ourselves of what is sung in all the Chrismas songs :

« Glory to God in the highest. And on earth peace, good will toward men ! »

We shall add that after having seen and heard, we esteem that the Caodaists are truly men of good will.

To a question we asked him on the subject of the doctrine exposed in the pamphlet graciously handed to all visitors, expressed thus :

« Without being polytheist in fact, it is so in principle, for besides the official adoration of the Supreme God, it allows its believers the free veneration of other gods who have conquered their hearts ».

In effect, we remarked to His Holiness Phạm-công-Tắc, that in all the revelations made to men on the subject of the Divinity, it was an acknowledged fact, even to the occultists, that there was only one god, in three persons, called by the appellation of « Divine Triad ».

That's right, replied His Holiness Phạm-công-Tắc, but for us, God is :

« The Incommensurable, the Eternal, the Most High, the Absolute. He has no name ».

In our religion, the word « gods » that has shocked you, has not the heathen meaning you lend it, it simply designates spirits completely detached from matter and approaching the Most High as near as possible.

They are, in a way, saints.

The names of our Eternal are given him by every people and under different forms.

These different names separate humanity instead of uniting them, that is why we don't call him God, but the Most High, the Absolute, the Eternal.

To another question concerning Christ, the answer was also categorical :

« We don't seek to destroy Christ's doctrine, we come, on the contrary, to strengthen it, for it is impossible to deny the existence of Christ. Our efforts aim at preparing, by spirituality, the regeneration of the whole of humanity, which seems to have forgotten all the maxims of Christ, which if they had been followed, should have kept peace in the world.

Caodaism is the bridge cast over the deep chasm (that seemed impassable) separating Christ from Buddha, who was his Precursor, the harmony of whose doctrines, completing one another, is necessary to the union of the Occidental and Asiatic peoples, that fraternity may reign between them.»

We could only bow before so wise a saying, which, furthermore, corresponds to that of Christ.

« I am not come to destroy the Law, or the Prophets. I am not come to destroy but to fulfil. »

It is moreover strange to find that in recent years, in the whole world the number of men who take an interest in the Holy Scriptures, increases steadily. This need of belief is typical and is for us the tangible proof that the time foretold by Daniel and Saint John, when Christ is going to return to the earth to give to each his due, is near.

So, we can only rejoice in the work undertaken by Caodaism, that of bringing back to Christ, by a necessary transition, the lost sheep of the Far-East, in order that, according to Saint John :

« One shepherd and one flock »

« There shall be but one shepherd and one flock ».

Le Populaire d'Indochine (27-11-36) also had an interview with the Superior of Caodaism under circumstances as follows :

« A crowd estimated at some twenty thousand persons occupies the alleys, the gardens and the « woods » of TâyNinh since yesterday.

They have come from all parts of Cochinchina, some by boat, others by cart. They camp in the open air, men and women, seated on mats, near the big oxen that have brought them here.

TâyNinh is in holiday. TâyNinh is celebrating the end of mourning for the late Pope Lê-văn-Trung.

On the square of « Universal Fraternity » which is illuminated by the garish light of a sweltering sun, a big alter has been erected to the memory of the former Chief of Caodaism.

On this altar is stretched an immense cloth representing Mr. Lê-văn-Trung with his sacerdotal trappings.

From both sides of the gigantic esplanade which is the place of « Fraternity » are lined up, province by province, the delegations from the interior with their chiefs, banners, and oriflammes. A new rule established only since Mr. Lê-văn-Trung's death reduced the period of mourning to twenty months instead of twenty four.

But, for Mr. Lê-văn-Trung, the old rule was maintained.

While awaiting the great night festival, we went to pay a visit to Mr. Lê-văn-Trung's successor, Mr. Phạm-Công-Tắc in his small villa, at the very end of the alley « Thượng-Trung-Nhựt ».

Mr. Phạm-công-Tắc welcomed us with the delicate courtesy for which he is well known.

He gracefully answered all our questions :

« Have you come into communication with Mr. Lê-văn-Trung's spirit ?

— Yes, many times.

— By yourself or through a medium.

— Through a medium, though I am a medium myself, and could make direct contact with the late pope's spirit.

— What recommendations did he make ?

— To do our best to open our religion to all faiths, all beliefs, in broad spirit of tolerance, to destroy the materialist error wherever we shall meet it.

— Tell us of the work of propaganda of Caodaism abroad.

— It is not an easy work, for it is not proper to wound the susceptibilities of the nations to which we come.

For our propaganda in China, the members of the mission are already named, but they are at present finishing their cultural formation in the Seminary.

— How many Caodaist seminaries are there ?

— Two ; one at TâyNinh, the other at PhnomPenh. The government has suggested that we discontinue them. But that is not possible, for we must form true priests.

— Have you any Frenchmen in your religion ?

— Oh yes. Many Frenchmen are beginning to learn our religion by correspondence.

In France, Mrs Félicien Challaye bears the executive powers with the title of « Giáo-sư » (that is, bishop) while Mr. Gabriel Gobron carries the legislative powers with the title of « Tiếp-Dẫn Dạo-Nhơn » (i.e. instructor).

— What is the actual number of followers of Caodaism.

— At one time, the schism of Bến-Tre did our religion an injury which saw numerous faithful turn away from it. But now, we have reached nine tenths of the number of followers we had at the moment of the greatest extension of Caodaism. The figure is more than one million.

« In Tonkin, we have between 6 and 7.000 faithful.

With these words, we take leave of Mr. Phạm-Công-Tắc, because many other callers wish to talk with the pope.

From 7 o'clock in the evening on, the gardens of TâyNinh are illuminated by thousands of Chinese lanterns, while paper images representing genii are illuminated by soft lights.

A spotless moon gives this ceremony a somewhat unreal character.

Ten thousand of the faithful already occupy the spots reserved to them in the parade of the great procession.

And one cannot deny that a certain mysticism emanates from that quiet moon-white train, from that endless parade under big trees that not the least breeze stirs nor the least cry disturbs.

Caodaism, among its other adversaries, has also met certain spiritualists, in spite of its origin of spiritualistic practises (at least, in the qualified Sacerdocy). It seems that spiritism is a new wine that bursts old bottles : a mass of followers having understood nothing of the explosion of spiritism in our ultramodern world, have squabbled and disputed with one another to know whether it is a philosophy, a science, a religion, without knowing (or without wishing to know) that it is all these at the same time and does not bear that artificial compartmentalizing of pedants and illiterates.

We then have religious spiritualistic countries (Great Britain, Brazil, etc.) and scientific spiritualistic countries (France, Italy, Cuba, Argentina, etc.). Better : in the same country, we find groups with a religious tendency (Christic spiritism in England, France, etc.) and associations with a scientific tendency (Revue Spirite at Paris, Revue Spirite Belge at Liege, etc.)

Scientific spiritualists, in general, are hostile to Caodaism, which they reproach for its ceremonies, rites, sacerdocy, « catechisms », and at the slightest provocation, those good apostles would excommunicate it without a trial ! I know what I say in writing these painful observations.

They would have an Asia more Voltarian than Voltaire ! Such ignorance is not encouraging...

Mr. Phạm-công-Tắc, Superior of Caodaism », wrote to me, on the 25th of March 1935, from the Holy See at TâyNinh (Cochinchina), a letter that I publish, not for the flattering appreciations it contains about me (perhaps, you will believe me if I confess this : I have not yet come to work impersonally, anonymously, as every advanced Initiate ought to work for social service, but I have come to an absolute indifference before praises and blame expressed about my work and me), but for certain teachings, for certain precisions which it contains :

« My dear Brother,

« Our Brother, Mr. Vinh, has shared with me all your letters as well as your articles appearing in various reviews.

« Allow me to thank you with all my heart for busying yourself with the new Doctrine with such a noble self-sacrifice Our Divine Master holds you in great consideration, and we pray that He may give you better health to be able to continue without interruption the work you have so well undertaken. This very evening, I am going to conduct divine service and present to that end a petition to our Divine Master. Do believe that I have been very sorry to hear that you are suffering and that, from time to time, illness confines you to your bed. You must be well to work. Man has but few years to live on this earth of trials, and time is precious to him, very precious, when he knows how to use it.

Humanity lives in suffering. It is our duty to seek, by all means, if not to end those sufferings, at least to relieve them. So long as we draw a breath of life, let us work, always work for the regeneration of man, his perfection, the fraternization of races, the universal peace, that so much promised (and so little realized) peace.

Thanks to your unwearying activity that you have made known the new Doctrine in numerous spots of various countries. I beg you to persevere in your task, for I am firmly convinced that one day soon, your efforts shall be crowned with success.

I am sure that our Divine Master and numerous spirits watch over you and inspire you marvelously.

Always keep in close and regular relations with spiritualistic circles and help their members understand that, by the divine Will, we Cochinchinese, have but a little mission that limits itself to the creation of a Sacerdocy to whom we inculcate a *Faith*, a great *Faith* in God, and it needs the gathering of all spiritualistic messengers of the whole world to prepare the New Gospel capable of renovating the World in the way of Truth; in order that man may walk no more in darkness and that he may know where he comes from, what he is doing in the present life, and what he will become after death.

You are very specially named for that great task. God made you a polyglot for the purpose. You have that great advantage over all of us here, who, besides our mother tongue, speak and write French but imperfectly.

I know that Spiritualists have among them immutable principles; they do not want religion, nor cumbersome rites, it will be very difficult to make them admit our ideas and accept our new

Faith. But I have confidence that God and the spirits will help you in this difficult task, and when the time comes, their Great Master Allan Kardec, will manifest himself to bring them back towards us. The Spirit Victor Hugo, under the pseudonym « Symbol », has sent them several messages.

« On the other hand, Brother François of PhnomPenh has shared with me his answer to Brother Henri François, of France. I fully approve of its terms... I am pleased to quote : « Intellectuals, scholars are generally carried to extremes : they are either atheists or believers, sometimes to the point of intolerance, not to say fanatism. Let us follow in the Golden Mean, as the sage Confucius recommends. »

« Here-inclosed is the translation of a message our Brother Cao-đức-Trọng (Tiếp-Đạo) and I have obtained from Victor Hugo's Spirit, concerning dignitaries of Hiệp-Thiên-Đài Please read the explanations given on this subject to Brother Henri François by his name-Sake of Cambodia.

« I think that you have been solicited by many persons as to how we shall succeed in unifying all Religions which, by their principles, dogmas, rites, beliefs, etc... are so clearly different, even opposing and contradicting one another, not to say posing as adversaries.

« We might answer by these few sentences which, in my opinion, explain the question quite clearly in spite of being somewhat laconic.

« Let us consider Religions as departments of a University ».

« To be admitted into one of these departments, a student must first have his B.A., a key giving him access to the University of his choice.

« To have his diploma, a student must pass through the primary and elementary classes and so on, where he must acquire a sufficient range of diverse, even heterogeneous knowledge.

« To form a University, there must be Several departments. Each department has its particular teaching, but all must be under one leadership : a president.

« Broad acquired knowledges will always be useful to the student in the future and give him the stamp of a learned man. In the department of his choice, he must improve the studies of his choice, but the others already acquired are not useless at all. An engineer is versed in mathematics, a physician anatomy, a lawyer must be schooled in the law, but each of them has to know, in addition, letters, figures, a little of other matters, always necessary in life.

« In spite of their particular knowledges, their professions, they cannot live outside society.

« So, society re-unites them after their graduation. More-over, the engineer cannot get along without the physician, nor the physician without the engineer.

« It is the same with religions.

« A lay man must have acquired some principles of morals, some notions of philosophy, etc. to be well thought of, and not be expelled from Society. He thus prepares himself for entry into a religion to his taste.

« Religions are like University departments : superficially their dogmas, beliefs, ete... seem to be out of harmony with one another, they often are in opposition. They must be so, for each one has a taste, a tendency, a desire, an instruction, an education completely different of that of his neighbour.

« Religions were differently created because of the stage of civilization of peoples, the degree of evolution, the atmosphere, place of their birth, their manners and customs, etc. But above all these things, seeming so diverse, there is the Creator, God, i.e. the Universal Conscience who unites all men in spite of the diverse colours of their skin, their degree of civilization, etc...

« It belongs to the Caodaists to place themselves at the service of the «*Great Faith in God*» for that «*Union*» that will put an end to the terrible «*nightmare*», fratricidal world war, by which men are obsessed and which is even now being prepared so actively in Europe.

« Dogmas, and sectarianism confine man to a very reduced circle, where he sees only too small a part of the solar world that enlightens him. He must evolve. So, he must seek to know, to progress, in order not to mark time. Religion must not be for him like a cord that encircles a child who already knows how to walk, but whose nurse, obtuse or unreasonably fearful of her responsibility, still holds strongly in her hands, under the pretext that the child may lose his balance and fall.

Present humanity is pretty a « big child » to be held in leash and prevented longer from marching toward the Sublime. He needs the open air of the Infinite to be in conformity with the state of his soul and his devotion. He ought to be able to act and live in Truth, not darkness, or obsessed and obsessing doubt.

Hoping to hear from you soon, I leave you with a hearty embrace begging God to cover you with his benediction and graces, and asking you to give my best regards to our dear sister, Mme Gabriel Gobron.

Phạm-công-Tắc

Superior of Caodaism

Holy See of TâyNinh

As one can see, it is to the contributor to the Revue Spirite (Paris) as well as the Caodaist instructor that His Holiness speaks. Though we have suffered disagreeable rebuffs, in certain spiritualistic circles, we must heartily thank our friend, Mr. Hubert Forestier, Editor-in-Chief of the Revue Spirite, who has never made any objection to the insertion of a « paper » designed to establish confidence in the brethren of Vietnam, helping them to emerge from their martyrdom. On the contrary! He has always been happy to intervene on their behalf, especially to facilitate my task, in certain International Spiritualistic Congresses (Barcelona

1934, Glasgow 1937), and give the widest publicity to certain documents in favour of Caodaism.

In theosophical circles, the same understanding, in general, in spite of certain anticaodaist elements, incapable of revising a once-cristallized judgment, and which have influenced other theosophists...

CONCLUSION

In the Service of Caodaism

I have given much of my life to Caodaism. I have shared its pain, its sorrows, its discouragements, at tragic times when doctors of philosophy and sons of hate were bullying it and persecuting it in hundreds of cynic or hypocritical ways. I have lived its joys, its hopes, its triumph, at happy moments when knights of the spirit and men of good will were granting it a truce or recognizing its right to more justice.

In spite of precarious health, I have made these sufferings my own ; they were sometimes added to my almost daily worries. To the trials of Caodaism were added, in a painful fraternity, my own karmic reparations. After overwhelming hopeless days, a ray of light has from time to time pierced the cloud, and the sun has swept the Ardennes fog. It was my health that, once more, recovered for a time ; It was some newspaper or letter which, by air or sea mail, brought from Indochina joyous news which made me exult.

For 13 years, I have thus lived the life of my brethren of Vietnam, making it one with my own.

I have regretted a thousand times having no more spiritual power, useful relations, talent and lucidity, in order to help them better in their constructive efforts as well as in their silent distresses. I would do much for them, and I feel, in all humility, that I have done very little ! Forgive me, my good, my kind Vietnamese brethren, for having been so little the Instructor in France that you solemnly named, for having been only the humble follower you familiarly call :

« Brother Gago »

Rethel, 1937 - 1938 — Nancy, 1939

APPENDIX

Appendix

APPENDIX

About Mr. Chiếu, the first Caodaist, *la Revue Caodaiste* (N° 22, March 1933), on the occasion of his disincarnation, brings us some details.

1. — *His childhood*

The Phủ Ngô-văn-Chiếu was born on the 28th of February 1878 at Bình-Tây (Chợ-Lớn) in a modest house situated behind the pagoda dedicated to Quan-Đế, the Chinese Turenne.

At birth, he refused his mother's breast, and had to be given, instead of natural milk, rice soup.

His parents who were very poor, later came to live at Mỹ-Tho, and commended him to the care of his aunt, who sent him to school. Endowed with a quick intelligence, he soon was conspicuous and, when at twelve, he presented himself to the Administrator of the province of Mỹ-Tho to solicit a scholarship ; it was granted. Admitted as a scholarship boarding student, first at primary school, then at the college of Mỹ-Tho, he worked earnestly and passed with sussess his competition for a government position. At that time, this envied position was the crowning touch to a French-Vietnamese secondary education. Aged 21 years, the young man contented himself with it, for want of being able to carry his study further, and in order to help his parents.

II. — *His life as an official, and his religious vocation.*

The new official was appointed to the Immigration Service, at Saigon. He spent three years there, from 1899 to 1902. Having a natural tendency for religious things, he liked to tell the stories of saints and adventures of the immortals of antique China that he had heard narrated by Chinese comrades, when he was at his aunt's, who was married to a Chinese. One day, one of his friends surprised him relating a tale of saints to some little Chinese pupils at Chợ-Lớn, to whom he gave private lessons every evening. He had a great respect for genii and saints. At home he had erected an altar in honour of Quan-Thánh Đế-Quân. He often recited the « Minh-Thánh-Kinh », a book of prayers whose author was the spirit of that great general, a man of high virtue, who fasted two days per month.

In 1902, during a spiritualistic seance that took place at Thủ-Dầu-Một, where he was present, a superior Spirit was manifested and, after having revealed to him his future religious mission, advised him to practise the Đạo without delay.

TABLE OF CONTENTS

Editor's note	3
Introduction by D.G.	7
Origins of Vietnamese spiritism	17
Fundamental principles	33
Caodaism and Victor Hugo	51
What are the Caodaists ?	59
Caodaism at the international Congresses	63
Popes of Caodaism	71
Inauguration of the Caodaist Temple of PhnomPenh	79
Doctrinal precisions	99
Caodaist ritual	121
Spiritual directions (Extract of a letter)	141
Caodaism and its various branches	149
Caodaism, a state Religion, the national Religion of Vietnam	159
What His Eminency Trần-quang-Vinh thinks of	163
Essential elements of Caodaism	167
Some words from the Holy See	171
Conclusion : In the service of Caodaism	183
Appendix	185

CHINH-PHỤ NGÂM

1. — Thuở trời đất nổi cơn gió-bụi,
2. — Khách má-hồng nhiều nỗi truân-triên.
3. — Xanh kia thăm-thẳm từng trên,
4. — Vì ai gây-dựng cho nên nỗi nầy ?
5. — Trống Tràng-Thành lung-lay bóng nguyệt,
6. — Khói Cam-toàn mờ-mịt thức mây ;
7. — Chín lần gươm báu trao tay ;
8. — Nửa đêm truyền hịch đợi ngày xuất chinh
9. — Nước thanh-bình ba trăm năm cũ.
10. — Áo-nhung trao quan-vũ từ đây.
11. — Sứ trời sớm giục đường mây,

The verses of ĐẶNG-TRẦN-CÔN, artistic in form and of incomparable harmony, are strictly classic. They had a great influence on the poetry of the latter Lê dynasty.

At the beginning of the LÊ-CẢNH-HƯNG period (1740), many wars broke out in Việt-Nam. Soldiers set out on distant expeditions from which they never returned. The author, seeing the sorrow of separation, vexed his poetic soul with that grief which inspired him to compose this plaintive ballad on behalf of a warrior's wife

His work was widely read, and pronounced a masterpiece by his country-men. It was then translated into the vernacular by ĐOÀN-THỊ-ĐIỀM born in the village of Hiến-Phạm, subprefecture of Văn-Giang, BắcNinh province. With the pseudonym of Hồng-Hà, this woman of letters compared herself to the « rosy-glow ». She lived under the 18th-century latter Lê dynasty, and early in life showed literary endowment. At the age of fifteen years, she had acquired a great reputation.

She was married in her thirtieth year to a writer of great renown, Nguyễn - Kiều, born in Từ - Liêm, and better known under the pseudonym of Hạo-Hiên. After her husband's death, ĐOÀN-THỊ-ĐIỀM replaced him as a professor. Her teaching was in great demand, and many among her students became officials of high standing. She died in her 70th year, crowned with glory.

From the work of the poet ĐẶNG-TRẦN-CÔN, the learned woman, with all her talent and heart, realized in the national language a nearly perfect translation. Having undergone the proof of time, its splendor shines ever purer. By its singular charm, and the rare elegance of its style, it now appears as one of the finest jewels of our literature. By an irony of chance ĐOÀN-THỊ-ĐIỀM's translation has completely dethroned the original poem, which has, nevertheless, its own perfection of clarity and polish.

PHẠM-XUÂN-THÁI

PREFACE

The original text of the poem Chinh-Phụ-Ngâm was written in Chinese characters by ĐẶNG-TRẦN-CÔN, born at the village of Nhân-Mục (*commonly called Mọc*); subprefecture of Thanh-Trì, Hà-Đông province.

The poet was born under the latter Lê dynasty when Lord Trịnh-Giang was the true Chief of Government (1729-1740).

In his early years, he showed a passionate desire for study, and often sat up late by the dim light of an oil lamp.

At that time, as conflagrations had been frequent in Thăng-Long, the imperial city (*now Hanoi*), the Government forbade the use of lights in urban houses. This deprivation of his studious lamp forced him to dig an excavation to carry on his precious studies.

He received his Hương-Cống (*M.A. degree*), was appointed Huấn-Đạo and later a member of the Council of Censorship. He had a taste for liberal life. alcohol, and poetry. He cared little for the monotony of rites and ceremonies.

PHẠM-XUÂN-THÁI

WARRIOR'S WIFE'S

Plaintive Ballad
(CHINH-PHỤ NGÂM)

MCMXLVIII

TỨ - HẢI
PUBLISHING - HOUSE
112 Gialong, SAIGON

TỨ-HẢI Publishing-House

PHẠM-XUÂN-THÁI

WARRIOR'S WIFE'S PLAINTIVE BALLAD
(Translation of a famous Vietnamese poem)

VIETNAMESE - ENGLISH CONVERSATION DICTIONARY

REFORMED VIETNAMESE WRITING

PHILOSOPHICAL LEXICON
(Vietnamese-French — French-Vietnamese
German-English — English-Vietnamese)

TỨ-HẢI — 112, Gia-Long — Saigon-Vietnam

PRINTED ON THE PRESSES
OF THE LÈ-VĂN-TÂN
PRINTING-HOUSE, 49-59
RUE AMIRAL DUPRÉ,
——— SAIGON ———

Authorization N° 333/T. X. B. Saigon, September 12, 1950.

VARRIOR'S WIFE'S PLAINTIVE BALLAD

1. — In time of devastating war,
2. — The gentle sex is submitted to many misfortunes.
3. — The Blue Sky being too far above us,
4. — Who would be the Author of this very circumstance ?
5. — The Great Wall's drum glitters in the moonlight ;
6. — Cam-Toàn's smoke darkens the clouds.
7. — The King commits the emblem-sword to the Expedition's Commander ;
8. — At midnight the latter promulgates the royal edict fixing the day for marching to the battle field.
9. — The country was in peace three hundred years ago,
10. — Now the officers are going to wear again their uniforms.
11. — As the royal messenger speeds their departure,

PHẠM XUÂN THÁI

DANH TỪ TRIẾT HỌC

(VOCABULAIRE PHILOSOPHIQUE - PHILOSOPHICAL LEXICON)

VIỆT - PHÁP   ANH - VIỆT
VIỆTNAMIEN   ANGLAIS
FRANÇAIS   VIỆTNAMIEN
VIETNAMESE   ENGLISH
FRENCH   VIETNAMESE

PHÁP — VIỆT — ANH — ĐỨC
FRANÇAIS — VIỆTNAMIEN — ANGLAIS
ALLEMAND — FRENCH — VIETNAMESE
ENGLISH — GERMAN

TỨ HẢI MCML

PREFACE

A nation's highest claim to glory is her contribution to the human patrimony of civilization and culture. Of this, our people is by no means incapable.

But to become a creator of culture, this nation must first make the universal culture accessible to her people. Now our elite has acquired its knowledge in a foreign tongue. Wishing to communicate it to our people, they are at a loss. Our language itself, systematically abandoned for half a century, needs to be brought up to date to fulfil its office. The difficulty is not insurmountable, but requires the greatest effort. By a happy chance of history, we find ourselves endowed with a language that can draw indefinitely upon its Chinese source for all needed terms, while being, by its form, a means of expression incomparably more convenient.

Dàoduy Anh, with his French-Vietnamese Dictionary, and Hoàng-xuân-Hãn, with his Scientific Lexicon, should receive due credit for having tackled these necessary works.

But besides the everyday language and scientific terminology, there is a vast domain : economy, politics, morals, religion — all that has ever been thought about man, life and the world, since there were men and they began to think — in a word, philosophy in its broadest sense. It is undeniable that this is the most authentic phase of culture, which a nation attains as it rises. Yet this is not a separate domain, apart from real life, as we can see in contemporary history imbued with ideology, and in current events, heavy with meaning. It is sufficient to witness the explosive power of such words as democracy, marxism, materialism, dialectics.

Our journalists, whose business it is to impart to the public facts and ideas of the world, know how hard it is to put these concepts into our language ; concepts difficult to understand and to define — but still more difficult to translate. Recognizing that a large part of this new vocabulary is coined according to the personal judgment of each writer, is it surprising that these concepts remain vague and misunderstood by the public.

Still more grievous, it often happens that the specialists do not agree among themselves, and in this field, how dangerous are confusion and equivocation.

The present work seems to us to offer an invaluable service. On the one hand, it will help to find heretofore missing words to translate important concepts of the universal culture. On the other hand, it can put an end to the present anarchy in this realm of vocabulary by fixing the definition of existing words.

Its title implies that it serves only declared philosophers. But we find here, not merely the terms of pure philosophy, but everything within the sphere of ideas. For this reason, it will be an indispensable tool for all Vietnamese who have received French training - almost all of us - who in their turn would like to initiate their countrymen into the realm of culture.

We know, further, a great many foreigners, French and others, who, stopped till now by the above handicaps, await impatiently a work such as this, which will enable them to unite with our people and our culture on this incontestably noble plane, the plane of the soul and the spirit. It was no doubt with this hidden thought that the author of this Philosophical Lexicon has made a synoptical work with, opposite the Vietnamese terms, their synonyms in the three main languages of culture.

But this preface is already long. We wish only to voice our admiration of the author's courage and competence, which, to carry out such a work, must represent solid philosophical culture, and an astonishing knowledge of Vietnamese, Chinese Characters, English (of which he is an uncontested master), French and German. Should some errors or gaps remain, can they not willingly be forgiven ? We have only gratitude for this immense service he renders to our culture.

LEVAN HAI, Ph. D.

www.ingramcontent.com/pod-product-compliance
Lightning Source LLC
LaVergne TN
LVHW041615070426
835507LV00008B/251